What Older Americans Think

What Older Americans Think

INTEREST GROUPS AND
AGING POLICY

CHRISTINE L. DAY

PRINCETON UNIVERSITY PRESS
PRINCETON, NEW JERSEY

Copyright © 1990 by Princeton University Press
Published by Princeton University Press, 41 William Street,
Princeton, New Jersey 08540
In the United Kingdom: Princeton University Press, Oxford

Library of Congress Cataloging-in-Publication Data

Day, Christine L., 1954–
What older Americans think : interest groups and aging policy / Christine L. Day.
p.   cm.
Includes bibliographical references.
ISBN 0-691-07825-4 (alk. paper)
1. Aged—United States—Political activity. 2. Aged—Government policy—
United States. 3. Pressure groups—United States.
I. Title.
HQ1064.U5D39   1990
305.26'0973—dc20   89-24384

This book has been composed in Linotron Sabon

Princeton University Press books are printed on acid-free paper,
and meet the guidelines for permanence and durability of the Committee
on Production Guidelines for Book Longevity of the
Council on Library Resources

Printed in the United States of America by
Princeton University Press,
Princeton, New Jersey

10 9 8 7 6 5 4 3 2 1

For my parents,
Bonnie *and* Leonard Day

CONTENTS

ACKNOWLEDGMENTS

MANY people have helped me through the writing of this book, professionally and personally. Raymond E. Wolfinger was my closest adviser and harshest critic throughout the project. Four other people read complete drafts of the manuscript, and I profited tremendously from their respective areas of expertise: Jeffrey M. Berry in interest groups and democratic theory, Neil Gilbert in social welfare and aging policy, Nelson W. Polsby in all aspects of American politics, and Henry J. Pratt in all aspects of the politics of aging. Dennis Chong and Joseph White read and commented on some parts of an earlier draft. All of these people offered many extremely helpful suggestions which have made this a better book. I followed their suggestions selectively—far too selectively, no doubt—and am solely responsible for any errors or omissions that remain.

Discussions with several colleagues, including Claire Abrams, Beth Boles, Dennis Coyle, Elizabeth Greenberg, Richard Keiser, Adrienne Jamieson, Victor Magagna, and Philip Mundo, helped me clarify my thoughts about the role of interest groups in American politics as I was writing. Charles D. Hadley, Steven A. Shull, and John K. Wildgen at the University of New Orleans, and Joseph Autin and Diane Kron at the UNO Computer Research Center were especially helpful as I was reanalyzing and revising. Rosemary Griggs and Mary Ellen Grace cheerfully helped with the finishing touches.

The State Data Program at the University of California, Berkeley provided data, employment, friendship, and all kinds of other support during the bulk of this project. I am especially grateful to Ilona Einowski, Ann Gerken, Fern Glover, Lyn Lake, and other fellow researchers and staff members at the State Data Program.

The Institute of Governmental Studies at the University of California, Berkeley provided financial and logistical support, as well as stimulating seminars and discussions, while I was researching and writing.

I owe a special debt of gratitude to the people involved in the politics of aging, in both private associations and government, who cheerfully agreed to be interviewed in the midst of their hectic work schedules. I promised them anonymity, and therefore cannot thank them by name here, but I appreciate all their time, information, knowledge, and experience.

What Older Americans Think

Introduction

OLD-AGE political organizations in the United States are thriving, and their memberships are expanding. There are more than one thousand aging-based groups in the United States at the national, state, and local levels, not including more than five thousand local chapters of national organizations. These organizations cover a wide range of policy priorities, tactics and strategies, ideological preferences, and informal partisan affiliations.

The elderly themselves are a rapidly growing and politically salient sector of the population. The sixty-five-and-over population grew twice as fast as the rest of the population during the last two decades, with the eighty-five-and-over group growing even faster. The older population growth will reach even higher proportions as the "baby boom" generation ages. As most of these older people retire, they have more leisure time for political activity, and many are indeed politically active.

Older people have enjoyed a wide variety of policy gains and program expansions during the past few decades, and have fared better than most other groups during the domestic budget reductions of the 1980s (e.g., Lammers 1983; Rauch 1987). Public opinion polls show the elderly to be a highly popular and legitimate recipient group. At the same time, some politicians and journalists are beginning to complain that the elderly are too powerful, and their programs too immune to the budget cuts necessary to eliminate the federal deficit (e.g., Longman 1985; Samuelson 1981). Politicians, journalists, and scholars, as a result, are paying increasing attention to aging-based political organizations.

How have old-age political organizations representing a diverse collection of people become such a visible political force? This book traces the evolution of elderly interest groups from their beginnings as part of a diffuse social movement, to stable organizations, to major policy actors—with an emphasis on the contemporary politics of aging. Citizen participation through mass membership organizations is the primary focus, although other interest groups dealing with old-age policy are discussed as well. The study links the three broad theoretical themes that dominate interest group research but are generally treated separately: (1) group origin and maintenance, (2) group power and influence, and (3) constituency representation by interest groups.[1]

V. O. Key (1961) observed that the connections are tenuous between public opinion, interest groups, and governmental institutions. To-day—following the advent of the "advocacy explosion" spawning thousands of new political organizations and the widespread use of mass communications techniques for political purposes (Berry 1984)—these connections are more complex than ever. But if interest groups are little understood, they are still widely disparaged. Politicians delight in claiming to represent "the American people" while chiding their opponents for "catering to the special interests." Such claims play on the sentiment that in the politics of interest groups, certain groups enjoy special privileges that are denied to other people.

Are organized interests selfish, narrow, and systematically biased? Or are they the most efficient, equitable, and democratic way of articulating concerns and involving citizens in politics? They are neither; interest groups do not exist in a political vacuum, and both stereotypes are too simple-minded. Voluntary associations are simply one part of the complex American political system, and they perform a number of important functions within that system—transmitting information between constituents and policy makers, integrating individuals into the political system, and mobilizing people around issues they may otherwise pass off as personal rather than political problems.

Political organizations are an important channel for focused, collective action. They provide "continuity and predictability to social processes that would otherwise be episodic and uncertain" (Wilson 1973:7). They remain on the political scene to replace or supplement social movements, helping to work out precise solutions to vaguely articulated goals, and protecting group-based political gains that have ceased to be prominent because they are now taken largely for granted (Hardin 1982: 208–10; Costain and Costain 1983: 214). They not only articulate citizen interests to government, but also socialize and provide political information to citizens, thus serving as intermediaries communicating in both directions (Berger 1981: 9–10).

The influence that interest groups have over policy, the factors leading to their creation and survival, and the accuracy with which they

[1] The "constituency" of old-age organizations in this study refers to all older Americans, not just organization members (who are referred to as the "membership"). I use this broader definition of constituency because most of these organizations claim to speak for the interests of older people in general, and because the organizations' grassroots lobbying efforts often extend beyond their own dues-paying membership.

represent citizens' interests are important to the study of interest groups in a democracy. This study of older Americans, and the interest groups that represent them, explores these aspects of group representation and political power.

THEORIES ABOUT INTEREST GROUPS IN THE UNITED STATES

Since the birth of the nation, groups have been a major focus of political discourse, recognized as both necessary and dangerous to democracy.[2] James Madison wrote in *The Federalist Papers* about the "mischiefs of faction," the danger of selfish interest groups working against the good of the community as a whole. Curtailing freedom of expression and freedom of association was a cure worse than the disease, Madison believed. Instead, the multitude of competing and overlapping interests, the republican form of government, and the checks and balances written into the proposed constitution, would help prevent any one faction from dominating the others.

Alexis de Tocqueville, the astute observer of early nineteenth century America during the Jacksonian era, noted the propensity of Americans to form associations—an important asset for preventing the "tyranny of the majority" or the rise of a despot in a democratic society. Tocqueville, like Madison, recognized the potential for divisiveness and anarchy in a faction-ridden society. What obviates these dangers in the United States, in addition to the diversity of competing and overlapping groups, is a deeply rooted political consensus, in which "differences of opinion are mere differences of hue" (1945: pt. I, chap. 10; see also Berger 1981: 21). This consensus, said Tocqueville, preserves the peaceful and legal activity of political groups, in contrast to Europe, where wider differences in opinion promote factional violence and authoritarianism.

Groups again became a major focus of political study in the twentieth century, beginning with Arthur F. Bentley (1908), who described all of government and politics as the interaction of groups. David B. Truman expanded the theory in *The Governmental Process* (1971), an exhaustive study of political group interaction, overlap, and competition. Organized political activity, according to Truman, arises when a group's interests are threatened or disturbed; but the multiple and often competing interests of group members temper and moderate or-

---

[2] Some recent useful texts with extensive literature reviews on interest group politics include Berry (1984), Ornstein and Elder (1978), and Schlozman and Tierney (1986).

ganizational behavior. Truman's book, first published in 1951, turned the focus of political science from the study of governmental institutions and formal laws to the study of dynamic political activity, giving rise to the pluralism that dominated the literature in the 1950s and early 1960s.

The existence and diverse influences of a wide variety of groups are central to the pluralist view of American politics, exemplified by the theoretical and empirical work of Robert Dahl during this period (e.g. 1956, 1961). Politics in the United States, according to the pluralist perspective, is characterized by dispersion of power at the elite and mass levels; competition and bargaining over specific, pragmatic goals; and responsiveness of decision makers to a broad range of interests and to the electorate at large. No single class or narrow elite dominates the political process (Polsby 1980; Garson 1978: 24; Berger 1981: 21). Pluralist theory and empirical studies contradict those of the elite and stratification theorists like C. Wright Mills (1956), who asserted that a few wealthy and powerful individuals dominate American politics.

Political scientists have continued to study groups through the 1980s, with many writers examining and describing the biases of group political activity. Those who deny that a ruling class or a power elite dominates America still perceive that broad classes of citizens lack influence in the policy process. Whether studying the number and types of interest groups, the internal dynamics of groups and membership incentives, or the influence of groups in the policy-making process, many scholars have reached the same general conclusion: interest group politics tends to favor narrow producer groups and affluent individuals. Broad and diffuse publics, and the poor or disadvantaged, on the other hand, seem to have a more difficult time organizing to influence public policy.

Scholars have found many reasons for the dominance of narrow, privileged groups, and for perpetuation of the status quo, in American politics. Small and affluent groups, business groups in particular, possess the wealth and insider status conducive to successful lobbying (Schattschneider 1960; Bachrach 1967). The fragmented nature of groups and of American political institutions promotes incremental policies and narrow goals over broad-based and innovative solutions, such as universal health care and social welfare (Bachrach and Baratz 1962; McConnell 1966). Decentralized political arrangements favor local producers over broad national constituencies (McConnell 1966; Kesselman 1982). Ambiguous laws and government subsidies for narrow, established interest groups offer these groups many opportunities to help direct policy implementation (Lowi 1979). All of these characteristics have enabled the existing private organizations to form al-liances with specialized congressional committees and administrative agencies, to further their mutual causes (Lowi 1979; McFarland 1987).

The organizational disadvantages of broad and diffuse constituen-cies exist at the individual level as well. Olson (1965) introduced the "collective action" problem based on rational choice theory. Rational, self-interested individuals have no reason to join mass-based political organizations merely for political reasons. They can enjoy the fruits of organizational success whether they participate or not; they can, in Olson's words, be "free riders." Retirees, for example, receive Social Security benefit increases whether or not they worked with the orga-nizations advocating the Social Security legislation. The motivation for organization membership, therefore, is the offer of individual incen-tives, not collective goods; political lobbying becomes simply "a by-product of whatever function this organization performs that enables it to have a captive membership" (Olson 1965: 132). Small groups with narrow, specific goals, on the other hand, are in a better position to organize members for political action. The probability of contrib-uting individually to the group's success motivates small-group members.

Subsequent collective action theorists have expanded on Olson's model to try to explain why collective political action might be rational after all. Margolis's social choice model (1982), for example, posits that each person's internal utility function contains both a self-interest component ("S-Smith") and a group-interest component ("G-Smith"). While S-Smith responds to the offer of individual selective benefits, G-Smith responds to the offer of group benefits, particularly if group ideology explains "how the goals the group seeks are actually in the interests of society at large" or of a "class of individuals who are . . . especially deserving" (Margolis 1982: 100).

Rationality need not always be individual or private. Muller and Opp's "public goods model" stipulates that people may "recognize that what is individually rational is collectively irrational—that if peo-ple like themselves were individually rational free riders, the likelihood of the success of rebellious collective action would be very small," and therefore "it is collectively rational for all to participate" (Muller and Opp 1986: 484). Collective rationality is enhanced for potential par-ticipants when " 'enough others' have already joined to make it via-ble" (Chong 1987: 34). Collective action is also more crucial when the public good is unobtainable privately—clean air, for example—than when a substitute for the good—public education, for example—is available through the private market (Hardin 1982: 73; McLean 1986: 386).

Upper and upper-middle classes still enjoy the organizational advantage, however, even assuming collective action is rational. Participation in Margolis's individual model is a superior good: as income increases, the fraction allocated to the group-oriented G-Smith also increases, relative to the resources spent on S-Smith's personal needs. S-Smith must eat, in other words, before G-Smith can contribute to the common good (Margolis 1982: 41). Collective goods such as clean air also tend to be superior goods; the wealthy can spend a higher portion of their resources on such benefits (Hardin 1982: 69).

How, then, do political organizations, especially those with broad and diffuse constituencies, emerge and survive? The answer, for proponents of "exchange theory," lies primarily in the efforts of group leaders, or "entrepreneurs" (Salisbury 1969; Weissman 1970; Wilson 1973). The exchange framework focuses on the market-like exchange of incentives for organization membership and participation. Like business entrepreneurs, political group leaders offer a variety of incentives, attracting members by appealing to their diverse motives and needs. The most widely used typology of incentives is that developed by Clark and Wilson (1961): material, solidary, and purposive. Material incentives are tangible, having monetary value, such as product discounts or publications; solidary incentives provide the opportunity to socialize with other group members; and purposive incentives provide the political or ideological satisfaction of supporting a cause. Selective incentives, therefore, need not be tangible or material; a member joining a group for intangible rewards may still fit into Olson's rational choice framework. Thus, free ridership is not as great a problem as Olson implied, even for large groups with largely noneconomic goals (Cook 1984: 412; Hansen 1985: 94; Moe 1981: 537).

Exchange theory helps to explain how lower-class or disadvantaged persons, with few resources and little time to contribute to political organizations, might still be induced to join and participate. Such people would be most likely to respond to material incentives "that are immediately and directly available and of high value to the recipients" (Wilson 1973: 64). Political incentives are most likely to attract lower-class participants if they are sporadic and require few verbal and technical skills, for example, mass rallies or parades (Weissman 1970: 93–94). Yet even entrepreneurs who successfully recruit lower-class members often have to be more responsive to their affluent members in planning political goals and strategies. Members who join principally for purposive reasons are the ones who pressure their group leaders on political matters—and these members tend to come from the middle and upper classes (Moe 1980: 74). Furthermore, "emerging and dependent social groups" are particularly vulnerable to manipulation by charismatic leaders, whose organizations are inherently unstable (Pinner et al. 1959: 275–79).

Interest groups are not dependent solely on membership support for their existence and survival. For many political organizations, membership size and contributions are less crucial to their survival than support from outside patrons, including private foundations, government agencies, and philanthropists. Indeed, many lobbying groups are "staff" organizations with patronage support and few or no real members (Berry 1977; Walker 1983). Many groups with constituencies that are broad, diffuse, and difficult to organize manage to survive with the help of such financial support, although these are not the only types of organizations that receive outside assistance. Thus, the increasing sources of patronage have contributed to the expansion of the interest group universe during the last few decades.

Patronage is not the only reason for interest group expansion in recent decades. Higher income and education levels, the growth of mass communications techniques, rising public expectations coupled with public skepticism toward major institutions, and the decline of political party organizations, also help explain the proliferation of interest groups (Berry 1984; Cigler and Loomis 1986; Gais et al. 1984; Moe 1981; Wilson 1981). Many of the new organizations are citizen and public interest groups, representing broad constituencies that had previously been largely unorganized. The number of organizations involved in many policy domains has increased as a result, making issue networks more open and fluid, and exposing many narrow producer interests to countervailing group power (McFarland 1987; Gais et al. 1984).

This development has led many observers to conclude that the organizational landscape today is more equitable and more representative of the population. This conclusion has been challenged on several grounds, however. Many of the purported public interest groups consist not of large and active memberships, but of a few professional activists operating out of a small office with little public input (Berry 1977; Vogel 1980–81). Many of the citizen groups claiming large memberships are centralized mass-mailing operations in which the members neither meet together nor participate in decision making (Hayes 1986).

Finally, the rise in citizen groups has been accompanied by the active counter-mobilization of business and economic interests, so that the balance of organized interests remains the same as before: "tilted heavily in favor of the advantaged, especially business, at the expense of the representation of broad publics and the disadvantaged" (Schlozman and Tierney 1986: 87). If the late E. E. Schattschneider could observe American politics in the 1980s, he would still have reason to proclaim, as he did thirty years ago (1960: 35), that "[t]he flaw in the pluralist heaven is that the heavenly chorus sings with a strong upper-class accent."

OLDER PEOPLE AS A "SPECIAL INTEREST"

Scholars, as we have seen, have found many reasons why political organizations and their activities tend to favor narrow and affluent interests. Disadvantaged groups lack the resources for effective mobilization and lobbying; broad and diffuse interests lack intensity, focus, and appeal to rational choice. Yet older people in the United States have overcome some of these organizational difficulties, to the point where many observers now ascribe an excess of power and privilege to the elderly. How well do the group theories and observations outlined in the preceding section explain the emergence and influence of old-age political organizations?

Interest group leaders have used both membership incentives and patronage support to overcome organizational difficulties, and both factors have been important to the creation and survival of organizations representing the elderly. Membership incentives, forming the basis of the exchange theory of interest groups, have been paramount, as several old-age political associations have amassed memberships numbering in the millions.

Policy makers attribute the political visibility and success of old-age organizations to two major resources: large, geographically dispersed memberships, and politically astute and knowledgeable group representatives in Washington. These two resources are related: lobbyists' expertise is all the more impressive to policy makers because it is backed by large and active memberships. This book examines the development of these resources and the organizational success of older Americans.

The data for this study consist of both public opinion and elite opinion data. The public opinion data come from several national surveys dealing with aging policy and other political issues. The elite opinion data come from interviews with fifty-four interest group leaders and staff members, congressional staff members, and administrative agency officials dealing with aging policy.[3] Most of the interviews were conducted at the national level, in Washington; a few were conducted at the state level, in California.

There are several traits that make aging-based organizations amenable to comparisons with, or generalizations about, other types of interest groups. Like most other categoric groups, older people share a number of common and collective interests, yet in other respects are highly diverse with conflicting needs. As Truman noted (1971: 210), all persons "in a complicated society have a wide variety of memberships in competing groups and potential groups," adversely affecting the stability and cohesion of any one group. Older people, having reached the age of their own or their spouses' retirement, face new and changing group identifications, while maintaining close ties with many other groups—religious, occupational, partisan, ethnic, and so on. Older Americans range widely in social status, health, income, education, and quality of life. At the same time, they share the concerns that accompany the changes later in life.

How did the elderly become a special interest? Chapter 2 discusses the emergence and development of old-age interest groups in the twentieth century. The third chapter presents findings on older Americans' attitudes toward aging policy issues. I compare their attitudes with those of younger adults, and examine the sources of disagreement among older people themselves. Chapter 4 addresses the success of old-age political organizations in attracting members, using exchange

[3] Interviews were conducted with leaders and staff members of the following organizations: the American Association of Retired Persons, the American Health Care Association, the Congress of California Seniors, the Gray Panthers, the National Alliance of Senior Citizens, the National Association of Retired Federal Employees, the National Caucus and Center on Black Aged, the National Committee to Preserve Social Security and Medicare, the National Council of Senior Citizens, the National Council on the Aging, the Social Security Department of the AFL-CIO, and the Villers Foundation. Members of the following congressional staffs were also interviewed: U.S. Senate: Finance Committee, Health and Social Security Subcommittees; Labor and Human Resources Committee, Aging Subcommittee; Special Committee on Aging. U.S. House of Representatives: Ways and Means Committee, Health and Social Security Subcommittees; Select Committee on Aging; personal staffs of Rep. William Boner (D-Tenn.), Rep. Claude Pepper (D-Fla.), Rep. Fortney Stark (D-Calif.). California state legislature: Senate Health and Human Services Committee, Aging Subcommittee; Assembly Committee on Aging and Long Term Care. Administrative agency officials who were interviewed included officials from the following governmental units: U.S. Administration on Aging, Federal Council on Aging, U.S. Health Care Financing Administration, National Institute on Aging, U.S. Social Security Administration, California Commission on Aging, California Department of Aging.

or incentive theory—the market-like exchange of incentives for organization membership and participation.

Chapter 5 begins with an examination of aging policy advances during the past few decades, resulting in a marked but uneven improvement in the economic and social well-being of older people. The second part of the chapter traces the evolution of interest group power within the aging policy network, noting the expansion and increased effectiveness of their direct and grassroots lobbying. Finally, chapter 6 addresses the question of constituency representation by old-age interest groups. Collectively, the old-age organizations cover a lot of ground, differing among themselves in style and focus while often presenting the image of a powerful, broad "gray lobby"[4] to policy makers.

Who really benefits from the political activities of old-age interest groups? The elderly have gained political and economic ground during the last few decades as their organizational activity has increased. Old-age interest groups have become their own best advocates; they are less dependent upon coalitions with other groups than they were a decade ago, and they are more sought after as coalition partners themselves. At the same time, their achievements have been uneven: older people have become more economically diverse even as they have become collectively better off. While old-age organizations have been instrumental in achieving collective benefits for the elderly, they have little control over the degree of inequality among older people, especially inequalities carried into old age from earlier years of life.

Although old-age political organizations are successful within the context of interest group bargaining, macroeconomic theory suggests that it is political parties, more than interest groups, that control the larger economic agenda (Cigler and Loomis 1986: 305; Berry 1984: 219–20). "The crucial dilemma surrounding the politics of old age," Estes has written, "is whether any disadvantaged group in society can gain access to the resource system without itself becoming a special interest" (1979: 230). The key to the dilemma lies in coalition building among groups. Interest groups may be effective, on their own, in expanding the political agenda or protecting certain interests. Political parties, however, are more effective in building broad, enduring coalitions and coherent policy programs that influence the degree of inequality and the distribution of resources in society. Old-age political organizations, as we shall see, have been active in coalition building, but most of them—like many interest groups in the United States—have been reluctant to align themselves with one party or another.

---

[4] Henry J. Pratt (1976) coined the term "gray lobby" in his book of the same title.

Interest groups, we noted at the outset, are one part of a complex political system, and cannot be examined in a vacuum. They must be examined in their relations with the public, their constituency, the political parties, other interest groups, social movements, and the institutions of government. This we will do with older Americans and their political organizations.

CHAPTER 2

The Rise of Old-Age Interest Groups

EVERYONE ages; barring catastrophe, everyone grows old. Aging is a continuous process, with no well-defined boundary between "old" and "not old." The elderly are highly diverse; indeed, there are more differences *within* age groups than *between* them. Older people have, throughout their lives, acquired other group affiliations and loyalties unrelated to their chronological age. Nor can the politics of aging be viewed as a polarized intergenerational conflict. Younger adults have older relatives and their own futures at stake; public opposition to government support of the elderly is minimal.[1] How, then, did the elderly become a "special interest"?

The emergence of the elderly as a special interest dates back to the early twentieth century. The history of the senior citizen movement and the rise of old-age political organizations is a history rife with change: changes in the social status of and attitudes toward older people, in the political power and composition of senior advocacy groups, and in policies and institutions dealing with elderly issues. These social and political transformations have given rise to two related controversies about the role of interest groups in old-age politics.

The first controversy concerns the relative value of the "social movement" and "interest group pluralism" perspectives as bases for examining the political activities of older people. The interest group pluralism perspective emphasizes the competition among groups seeking political outcomes favorable to a particular constituency; the social movement perspective stresses collective action that aggregates interests on a broader scale, superseding narrow group interest (Carlie 1969; Pratt 1976; Williamson et al. 1982: 12).

The second controversy in the literature concerns the relative importance of advocacy by older people themselves, in contrast to advocacy by other individuals and groups on behalf of the elderly. The interest group pluralism perspective emphasizes the actions of older people working in their own self-interest at the expense of other groups, while the "coalition formation" perspective stresses the collective political

[1] See chapter 3.

efforts of elderly and nonelderly groups together, for mutual advantage (Williamson et al. 1982).

By examining the history of the senior movement and the changes that have occurred, we can see that each perspective has explanatory power at different stages of that history. First, the social movement and interest group perspectives are not mutually exclusive. Many social movement theorists, in fact, describe a social movement as a series of stages culminating in the formation of interest groups (e.g., Mauss 1975; Pratt 1976: 54–55, 196; Williamson et al. 1982: 81–101). A typical movement begins with the erratic and disorderly expression of grievances or demands, often channeled by a populist leader; moves toward ad hoc organization and discussion of political solutions; and eventually reaches the stage of formal organization and "institutionalization." This institutional phase is characterized by stable political organizations, a large membership base, substantial economic and political resources, hierarchy and division of labor, and connections with government agencies and officials. Thus the membership organizations, rather than replacing a social movement, become a part of it.[2] This pattern fits the evolution of old-age politics very well. The amorphous senior movement of the early twentieth century has developed into an array of established and institutionalized political organizations.

The importance of building coalitions with other groups has also changed over time for the old-age political organizations. At the turn of the century, the older population was an ill-defined sector with few recognized common political interests. Even after older Americans became aware of their common interests, their own organizations remained secondary actors on aging issues for several decades. Today, the elderly represent a well-organized sector of major importance within the aging policy system. Nor is this the final stage of the evolution. Early signs of a political backlash against the elderly, expressed by some politicians and journalists, have nudged the old-age organizations toward building new coalitions with nonelderly groups. This time around, however, other groups recognize the primacy of aging-based groups as social welfare lobbyists, and they actively seek the old-age organizations as formal coalition partners. This, then, is the story of how one particular "special interest" has evolved within a complex society composed of many potential interest groups.

[2] See Freeman (1975) and Costain and Costain (1983) for a discussion of formal organizations within the women's movement.

THE EARLY YEARS OF THE SENIOR MOVEMENT:
1900–1940

Old age did not become a focus for political activity and a target of national policy in the United States until early in the twentieth century. Prior to the social insurance and old-age pension movements which preceded the enactment of Social Security in 1935, older people depended upon individual effort, private charity, and limited local government assistance for their economic needs. The U.S. government, which had covered many Americans under an expanded Civil War pension plan in the late nineteenth century, did not replace these pensions with more comprehensive coverage as the Civil War generation died off (Orloff and Skocpol 1984). By the end of World War I, the United States had been transformed from an agrarian society into one that was industrialized, urbanized, and bureaucratized. Accompanying social changes increased the independence of older people in some ways, but also rendered the efforts of individuals and private organizations less effective in meeting the elderly's needs. In addition, the status and private power of older people had eroded to some extent.[3]

The advent of large-scale organization, public and private bureaucracy, and industrial technology led to new emphasis on the value of youth and educational achievement, at a time when most older people had grown up in a rural setting with few advanced educational opportunities. Families became more mobile, and multigenerational households became less common. Some scientists, in the face of increasing life expectancy and a growing proportion of older people, advanced new theories about the physical and intellectual degeneration underlying the aging process. Old age thus became less an object of veneration and respect, more an object of ridicule and obsolescence.

The lives of older people in general changed in ways that were neither inherently positive nor negative, but that did require new ways of meeting their needs. Along with the increase in urbanization, industrial technology, and family mobility, came a gradual increase in age segregation, movement toward retirement and leisure at an earlier age, and an increase in aging group consciousness. The pressures that built up into an old-age pension movement therefore came from various sources: from industrial managers seeking to replace older workers with a younger, faster, and more educated labor force; from social service professionals and voluntary organizations concerned about the welfare of a growing older population; and from older people them-

---

[3] This section draws largely from Achenbaum 1978; Lubove 1986; Pratt 1976, chaps. 2 and 6; Williamson et al. 1982, chaps. 1 and 3.

selves, demanding greater economic security and a higher standard of living in a changing world. By the time of the Great Depression and World War II, aging had become a national "problem" demanding a federal "solution."

Organized Activities on Behalf of the Elderly

The United States in the nineteenth and twentieth centuries lagged far behind Western Europe in developing social welfare and social insurance programs. The American traditions of individualism and voluntarism promoted self-reliance, and discouraged both state interference in the economy and governmental support for needy groups. In other western countries, a more comprehensive and institutionalized social welfare system precluded the need for a separate old-age pension movement. In the United States, by contrast, a social insurance movement developed after the turn of the century, but it lacked both numbers and broad-based support. Its proponents called for protection against such risks as unemployment, illness, accidents, old age, and disability, arguing that protection is a right, not a matter for charity. Such insurance would be financed partially by contributions from workers and employers, but the government would take responsibility for enforcing the policy and contributing a share of the funds. Lacking the success and general acceptance of government-sponsored social insurance found in other countries, the movement in the United States gradually began to focus on the elderly as a key constituency (Lubove 1986: 2–3, 113–14; Holtzman 1963: 18–19; Williamson et al. 1982: 150).

Why did the issue of old-age security rise to such prominence within social politics by the 1920s? Four major factors are cited in the literature: (1) demographic and economic realities which, by the time of the Great Depression, resulted in an older population that was both much larger and poorer; (2) the realization by employers that Social Security and mandatory retirement could be cost-effective; (3) the efforts of certain groups and individuals in the new social insurance leadership; and (4) increasingly broad middle-class support for a social insurance policy that cut across class lines, aided the nonpoor as well as the poor, and reinforced the idea of individual and employer contributions as opposed to government handouts.

Between the mid-nineteenth century and the New Deal era, when Social Security was enacted, the elderly share of the population had risen sharply, while changes in the social and economic structures of industrial society had diminished older people's opportunities for employment and financial independence.

The proportion of persons sixty-five years and over had increased from 2.1 percent in 1850, to 4.1 percent in 1900, 5.4 percent in 1930, and 6.8 percent in 1940 (U.S. Bureau of the Census 1975: 15). At the same time, the proportion of older males in the labor force had declined steadily; elderly unemployment was well above the national average; and the poverty rate among older people was growing rapidly. By 1940, about 40 percent of people sixty-five years and over depended upon some form of public assistance, up from 23 percent in 1910 and 33 percent in 1920 (Williamson et al. 1982: 82). For the vast majority of the elderly poor, this dependence meant moving to the poorhouse. By the time of the Great Depression, conditions were so desperate for older people—and for younger people with older parents and relatives to support—that governmental and public concern for the plight of the elderly had expanded the support for an old-age economic security system (Achenbaum 1978: 109–27; Lubove 1986: 113–14; Holtzman 1963: 23–24).

The second reason for the rising prominence of old-age security as a social issue was the growing awareness among employers that they, too, could benefit. Support for old-age retirement and pension systems grew among industrial managers and employers, not only for humanitarian reasons, but because of the growing perception that older workers lacked the stamina, dexterity, and technical knowledge of their younger coworkers. The number of private industrial pension plans had greatly increased by the 1920s, perceived as a business expense for the purpose of retaining the loyalty of superior workers and then letting them go as their productivity declined. Pension plans in the private and public sectors provided the groundwork for Social Security legislation mandating government involvement and compulsory insurance (Katz 1986: 200–205; Lubove 1986: 130–32).[4]

The social insurance leadership during the two decades prior to the passage of Social Security was the third factor contributing to the old-age pension movement of the early twentieth century (see Lubove 1986; Katz 1986; Pratt 1976; Williamson et al. 1982). Three of the most active organizations campaigning for the adoption of old-age

---

[4] Organized labor, for the most part, opposed industrial pension schemes during this period because they perceived such schemes as a technique of labor control and as a deferred wage dependent upon company loyalty (see Lubove 1986: 129–30). By the 1940s, in contrast, organized labor began to play a leading role in old-age politics, promoting such issues as expansion of Social Security coverage and benefits and, later, Medicare (Pratt 1976: 30).

pensions in the 1920s were the American Association for Old Age Security (AAOAS), the American Association for Labor Legislation (AALL), and the Fraternal Order of the Eagles. The AALL, headed by two economists, John Commons and his protégé John Andrews, advocated collective bargaining between business and labor to establish insurance plans for unemployment, injury, and retirement. The state, the AALL leadership believed, should require employers to create reserve funds for this purpose. The Eagles lobbied extensively in state legislatures during the 1920s for old-age pension plans; the resulting state legislation, though meager, helped set a precedent for government responsibility for old-age security.

The AAOAS, founded by Abraham Epstein in 1927, embodied many of the ideas advanced by social insurance expert Isaac Rubinow prior to World War I. It was Epstein who coined the term "social security"—he changed the name of AAOAS to the American Association for Social Security (AASS) in 1933—and who became a leading proponent of old-age security as a universal right. Epstein urged that government's primary goals should be income maintenance and redistribution, ensuring a comfortable standard of living for even the poorest of the elderly. At the same time, he adopted an approach that coupled government relief with employer and worker contributions, thereby softening policy makers' charges that Social Security was too "radical" or "socialistic."

The fourth reason for the rising prominence of the old-age security issue was the increasingly broad public support for the social insurance principle, and for universal, rather than means-tested, benefits. The distinction between *social insurance*, on the one hand, and *public assistance*, with its means-testing and its "welfare" stigma on the other hand, has been the key to public support for Social Security since its inception (Katz 1986; Brown 1984; Lubove 1986; Stockman 1987: 197–210). Social Security rests on the myth that workers "earn" their right to benefits by paying into the insurance system directly out of their paychecks, even though most Social Security recipients draw out much more money in benefits than they ever paid into the system.

In fact, Social Security was designed to balance two distinct goals: *equity*, or benefits based on the amount that an individual has paid into the system during his working life, and *adequacy*, or redistribution of income to protect against poverty and to help lower-income persons (Light 1985: 39; Lubove 1986: 180). Both Social Security and Medicare—as opposed to Supplemental Security Income and Medicaid, which are means-tested—are generally thought of as contributory insurance programs rather than as pay-as-you-go intergenerational transfers, and therein lies their popularity with the general public.

In the years preceding enactment of Social Security, the elderly emerged as a legitimate and popular "welfare group," in part because people realized that they would all eventually reap the benefits. The old-age security issue cut across class lines. Rich and poor, white- and blue-collar workers, caring for elderly relatives and looking forward to their own retirement, could all recognize the self-interest aspect of the plan (Katz 1986). By the time of its passage in 1935, then, Social Security enjoyed the support of an active and dedicated social insurance leadership, many employers and business managers, and, increasingly, much of the public at large.

Organized Activities by the Elderly

What role, if any, did older people themselves play in the old-age security movement of the early twentieth century? Some mass membership organizations of older people did become active in the 1930s, during the Depression, but their influence upon aging policy remains a matter of controversy. These organizations have been characterized as radical, charismatic, inflammatory, and not sufficiently pragmatic to lobby the government effectively. Nevertheless, they may have helped to keep old-age security on the political agenda, made less radical alternatives seem more palatable and feasible to policy makers, and provided the initial momentum for aging-based political organization later in the century.

California was the hub of grass-roots aging-based political activity during this period (see Fischer 1979; Pratt 1976: 23, 98; Williamson et al. 1982: 83–85). The unemployment rate for elderly Californians was higher than for the nation as a whole, and so was the proportion of persons sixty-five years of age and over. In 1920, 5.8 percent of Californians were in this age group, as opposed to 4.7 percent in the United States; in 1930 the percentages were 6.4 in California, 5.4 in the United States; and it was not until the 1960 census that the percentage of older people in the country as a whole surpassed that of California (8.8 percent in California, 9.2 percent in the United States) (U.S. Bureau of the Census 1975: 25). Many of these older Californians were migrants, lacking traditional family and hometown support enjoyed by more older people in other states. The older population was most highly concentrated in many California towns. This is where populist leaders of old-age pension movements found a following, and this is where the political mobilization of older people in their own behalf began.

Upton Sinclair, the muckraking novelist and politician, proposed a $50 per month pension for Californians over age sixty as part of his program to "End Poverty in California" (EPIC) in 1933. Sinclair ran as the Democratic candidate for governor on the EPIC platform in 1934, but was defeated and discredited by conservative Democrats and Republicans who gave EPIC the label "end poverty, introduce communism." Another organization, founded by radio announcer Robert Noble and known widely as the "Ham and Eggs" group, proposed that weekly pensions be issued in California, under the condition that the pension money be spent within one year. This plan was to stimulate the Depression economy through forced spending at the same time that it aided the elderly and the unemployed. The Ham and Eggs group, though rather short-lived, boasted a peak following of 300,000, and it publicized the pension issue through radio programs, rallies, and mass marches.

The largest and most visible Depression-era elderly mass organization, by far, was the Townsend movement (see Holtzman 1963). In 1933, Dr. Francis Townsend wrote a letter to the editor of his home-town newspaper in Long Beach, California, outlining a plan to aid Americans who were, like himself, over sixty. The plan called for a $200 per month pension, to be spent within thirty days in order to boost the economy, and to be financed through a national sales or "transaction" tax. The letter received an avalanche of response and spawned an organization that lobbied nationally for the pension, sponsored national candidates, and set up Townsend Clubs for older people throughout the country. At its peak in the mid-1930s, the Townsend organization claimed a membership of two million, or over 10 percent of Americans over sixty years of age. The plan's mass appeal was based on its simplicity and concreteness, its promise of hope to an older population devastated by the Depression, and its ideological mixture of radicalism (the large pension) and conservatism (the regressive tax). The clubs, in addition, offered friendship, sociability, and a sense of purpose to their members (Holtzman 1963: 40–56).

The Townsend organization's membership and support declined rapidly after the passage of the Social Security Act. Although Social Security did not even come close to providing the income security proposed by the Townsend plan, it filled some of the needs that prompted Townsend's mass appeal. Other reasons for the organization's demise include the plan's lack of pragmatism and compromise, the end of the harsh economic conditions of the Depression, the death of many members, the dwindling recruitment effort, the technical incompetence of its lobbyists, and the singular, charismatic leadership lacking structural continuity (Holtzman 1963: 200–205). Yet the elderly had become a new political force in the United States, one that would resurge by the 1960s.

How much influence did old-age mass organizations exert on the politics of Social Security early in the twentieth century? Holtzman (1963) contends that these groups, and the Townsend movement in particular, accelerated the passage of Social Security by dramatizing the plight of the elderly, shaping public opinion in the belief that old-age security was a right rather than charity, and posing a political threat sufficient to prompt policy makers to support at least a more moderate old-age security plan.

Other writers acknowledge the widespread appeal of the Townsend movement, but most portray the elderly mass organizations as peripheral actors, at best, in the old-age pension politics of the 1920s and 1930s. These organizations were personalistic and charismatic, lacking in organizational structure and funds, and tied to the espousal of panaceas rather than pragmatic legislative solutions. Their members' loyalties were divided and fleeting, and their memberships were concentrated in the western part of the country. The lion's share of influence upon the design and advocacy of Social Security came from sources other than the elderly membership organizations, including social insurance organizations such as AAOAS and AALL, industrial managers, and advocates within the government (Carlie 1969: 261; Lammers 1983: 37–38; Vinyard 1978: 28; Pratt 1976: 6–7). Some historians of the early twentieth-century pension movement do not even mention the elderly mass membership organizations (e.g., Lubove 1986).

Most observers, therefore, would characterize the old-age politics of the early twentieth century as fitting into the coalition formation framework. The political gains enjoyed by the elderly during this period were accomplished not by organizations of older people alone, but by other groups and individuals working in their behalf.

The old-age organizations that did exist, furthermore, displayed the features of social movements: populist leadership, failure to provide for leadership succession, lack of pragmatism and reluctance to compromise on policy proposals, failure to establish connections with government officials, and ultimately, the inability to survive a partial victory: the passage of the Social Security Act. The senior movement did evolve into the formal organization stage, but not before several years of near dormancy.

BETWEEN EARLY SOCIAL MOVEMENT AND FORMAL ORGANIZATION: 1940–1960

Whatever the impetus behind Social Security, its passage marked the beginning of the direct, institutionalized relationship between the federal government and the elderly. Older people were now an official beneficiary group, the clientele of government structures dealing specifically with their needs and demands. While the original Social Security legislation was rather modest in scope, it laid the groundwork for subsequent expansion throughout the next several decades, including the addition of survivors' and dependents' benefits, disability insurance, Medicare, and cost-of-living adjustments (Williamson et al. 1982: 86). Social Security was, in addition, merely the first of many programs and benefits for older people to come in the years ahead. Furthermore, the governmental agencies and officials of the aging policy system had a stake in the maintenance and expansion of their own programs. They not only performed services for the elderly, they also advocated in behalf of older people and attempted to mobilize their clientele to do the same (Walker 1983; Pratt 1976: 41).

The two decades following the passage of Social Security, however, witnessed a marked decline in organized political activity by older people—a period that Pratt (1976) has called the "dismal years." The only significant elderly activity during the 1940s and 1950s was another California organization, George McLain's California Institute for Social Welfare. McLain claimed over one hundred thousand adherents and credit for increased old-age pension expenditures in California. His organization, however, was dependent on McLain's exclusive leadership, and lacked the structure, technical skills, and interpersonal relationships important to its continuity (Pinner et al. 1959; Pratt 1976: 34). Was the enactment of Social Security responsible, in part, for the dormancy of the senior movement during these years? Some writers maintain that this is indeed the case.

The Social Security Act of 1935, because of its initially limited scope, lack of health insurance, regressive payroll tax, and failure to significantly redistribute income to the most needy aged, was a disappointment for many old-age pension crusaders. At the same time, some observers feel, its passage defused the aging movement. The movement lost momentum once the federal government had responded, however inadequately, to the one major issue: old-age income security (Fischer 1979: 60; Holtzman 1963: 211; Williamson et al. 1982: 86–88).

The "political economy" view of aging politics takes this argument a step further: Social Security and other programs targeting the elderly have reduced and moderated the collective political activities of older people, and continue to do so. Government policies have largely segregated the elderly, removed them from the labor force, labeled them as an official national "problem," and maintained their dependency status rather than increasing their autonomy and well-being. Programs designed to increase older people's participation in advisory councils have channeled their activity away from advocacy of redistributive policies that would help those most in need (Estes 1979; Evans and Williamson 1984).[5]

Paradoxically, then, the governmental structures dealing with aging-based programs are viewed alternatively as a boon and a detriment to old-age political activity. Freeman (1975) notes in her work on the women's liberation movement that "the correlation between movement strength and the development of policy in accord with its aims is at best a rough one" (p. 233). Sympathetic policy can either preempt or encourage group activity; unsympathetic policy can either mobilize group members or demoralize them. The relationship between government and older people, like that between government and women, is complex.

The senior movement, at any rate, did not die out during the "dismal years" of the 1940s and 1950s. The passage of Social Security may have defused the movement, but it also made older people an identifiable client group of government, setting the stage for future demands and political action. There was, in fact, a resurgence of aging-based political activity by the middle of the twentieth century, marked by the rise of large and stable organizations. In the following section we will examine the reasons for this resurgence and provide a brief overview of these advocacy groups.

THE EMERGENCE OF STABLE OLD-AGE POLITICAL ORGANIZATIONS: 1960–PRESENT

The expansion of the "gray lobby," after a hiatus of several years, has been phenomenal. By the early 1980s, according to a report by the Research Department of the American Association of Retired Persons, the number of organizations confined to elderly memberships or focusing on aging policy numbered around one thousand at the local, state, and national levels. Local chapters of national organizations, in addition, exceeded five thousand (Pratt 1983:146). Many of these groups, in contrast to the groups of the 1930s and 1940s, have been active for twenty or more years. Founded in the 1950s and 1960s, these groups have become increasingly policy oriented and politically active, while those emerging in the 1970s and 1980s have been political since their inception—lobbying government, educating their members, and attracting media attention.

Among the modern-day groups are the national mass membership senior organizations—the focus of this book. These include the Amer-

[5] This view will be examined further in the chapter on representation (chapter 6).

ican Association of Retired Persons (AARP), the National Council of Senior Citizens (NCSC), the Gray Panthers, the National Committee to Preserve Social Security and Medicare (NCPSSM), and the National Alliance of Senior Citizens (NASC). Also included, at the national level, are occupation-based retiree groups, the most prominent of which is the National Association of Retired Federal Employees (NARFE); organizations aimed at addressing the needs of particular categories of older persons, such as the National Caucus and Center on Black Aged, the Asociación Nacional pro Personas Mayores, the National Indian Council on Aging, the National Pacific/Asian Resource Center on Aging, and the Older Women's League; professional and service provider associations such as the National Council on the Aging, the Gerontological Society of America, the National Association of State Units on Aging, the National Association of Area Agencies on Aging, and the American Association of Homes for the Aging; and private philanthropies, the most prominent of which is the Villers Foundation.

The American Association of Retired Persons is the largest, by far, of the mass membership organizations. Its membership grows by millions annually, and by the late 1980s numbered over 28 million persons fifty years of age and over, or about one-third of Americans in that age group. Membership eligibility age was lowered to fifty in 1983, and today nearly 40 percent of its members are under sixty-five years old. One of the largest voluntary associations of any kind (Walker 1983), AARP is a multi-purpose organization, service oriented as well as political. It originated as the National Retired Teachers Association (NRTA), founded in 1947 by Dr. Ethel Percy Andrus, a prominent California educator. Dr. Andrus was less concerned with influencing policy than with raising the status and self-esteem of older people. Recognizing that older people often had trouble obtaining life insurance, she made arrangements with a leading insurance company to offer policies to NRTA members. The insurance program became so popular that retirees in other occupations began to ask for the same benefits, leading to the founding of AARP for all older people regardless of occupation.

Although AARP was chartered as part of NRTA in 1958, the two organizations soon merged and in 1982 became known simply as AARP. During this period, the insurance company handling AARP's membership health insurance benefits, Colonial Penn, had become highly profitable, with most of its business coming from AARP. By the mid-1970s, other insurance companies were also offering health insurance to older people, an untapped market before Andrus founded NRTA. Critics of Colonial Penn leveled two charges at the company: that Colonial

Penn's insurance policies offered less protection than alternative policies, and that the company was dominating AARP's political decision
making. According to the second charge AARP failed to support any
government health insurance programs, such as Medicare, that would
cut into Colonial Penn's market.

Criticism mounted through the late 1970s, until AARP broke relations with Colonial Penn, opened its insurance operation to competitive bidding, and accepted the bid from Prudential, which remains
AARP's health insurance underwriter. At that point, AARP's politics
moved to the Left, according to several leaders and staff members of
other old-age organizations. Most were reluctant to link AARP's pro-
liberal shift directly to the insurance company connection, but two interviewees did affirm the relationship. "They're less conservative since
the break with Colonial Penn," said one. "Prudential has less control
over AARP policy."

Today, AARP has a moderate-to-liberal political stance and a largely
middle-class, white-collar membership. The partisan and ideological
preferences of the members, according to AARP's own surveys, range
widely, as would be expected in such an enormous organization.
AARP's political activities and membership recruitment efforts have increased dramatically during the 1980s (Kosterlitz 1987c). In addition,
AARP has greatly expanded its list of low-cost member benefits and
services, including insurance and health aid discounts, mail-order
pharmaceuticals, travel services, investment opportunities, tax assistance, a magazine, newsletter, and special publications. The magazine,
Modern Maturity, now has a higher average circulation than any other
magazine.

AARP's paid staff of 1,300 includes a legislative staff exceeding one
hundred; its large, comfortable office building in Washington has a zip
code all its own. In addition to the paid staff, AARP's network of some
35,000 volunteer members includes national and regional officers as
well as local service and political committees. According to its newsletter, AARP's annual budget has reached nearly a quarter of a billion
dollars, one-third of which comes from membership dues and two-
thirds from related business and advertisement revenues.

The National Council of Senior Citizens, the second largest aging-
based organization with some 4.5 million members, was founded in
1961 with support from labor unions and the Democratic National
Committee. The organization arose out of the Democrats' Senior Citizens for Kennedy effort and the campaign to adopt Medicare legislation. NCSC, essentially an organization of over four thousand state and
local clubs and associations, retains its liberal Democratic bias and its

union ties. Its political action committee, established in the early 1980s, reflects its partisan affiliation. Most of its leaders are retired union members, and its membership consists largely of retired blue-collar workers, although in recent years it has worked to expand its appeal beyond its union base.

NCSC also offers its members an array of services including insurance and prescription discounts, travel programs, job retraining, and monthly publications, although not on AARP's grand scale. NCSC maintains a staff of 120, including researchers and lobbyists, in its cluttered Washington office. In addition to the lobbying, NCSC holds mass rallies and demonstrations to attract media and government attention— "street work," one NCSC staffer likes to call it. The organization is "more ideological" and "less cautious" than AARP, according to its staff—a characterization readily supported by policy makers.

The Gray Panthers, more radical in orientation than the other groups, was founded in 1970 by sixty-seven-year-old activist Maggie Kuhn, who opposed mandatory retirement and age discrimination in general. With its slogan "age and youth in action," the Gray Panthers organization originated as a coalition of older and younger people, and nearly half of its fifty thousand members are under fifty years old. The Gray Panthers have been less concerned with lobbying at the national level than with grass-roots organizing at the local level and mobilizing public opinion through demonstrations and other media events. They are, in fact, members of the only major national aging-based organization with headquarters located outside of Washington; the Philadelphia office has a paid staff numbering fewer than ten.

The Panthers' political goals emphasize radical social change over incremental policy changes; they have been active on such issues as poverty and nuclear arms reduction as well as old-age benefits. Their organization's decentralized structure delegates much political decision making to the one hundred local groups. However, they have also moved toward more national-level lobbying and a more hierarchical structure, recognizing to some extent the need to work within the system as well as against it, and to provide for continuity beyond the charismatic leadership of Maggie Kuhn (Jacobs 1980; Pratt 1983: 160–64).

At the other end of the ideological scale is the National Alliance of Senior Citizens, founded in 1974 by twenty-seven-year-old C. C. Clinkscales and now numbering over two million members. Conservative in orientation, NASC calls itself the organization for "responsible" senior citizens, and opposes most federal spending for old-age programs on the grounds that such spending will bankrupt the system and prove detrimental to older people in the long run. NASC runs a direct-mail membership drive from its suburban Washington office with a staff of ten, and it limits its lobbying to the national level. NASC also offers its members some publications and services, including a heavily advertised insurance plan. Its annual budget surpasses four million dollars—more than five times the Gray Panthers' budget.

The newcomer among elderly mass membership organizations is the National Committee to Preserve Social Security and Medicare, founded in 1982 by former Representative James Roosevelt, a California Democrat and oldest son of Franklin D. Roosevelt. Born at the height of the debate over the Social Security funding "crisis," NCPSSM quickly raised more than five million dollars and signed up more than half a million members through direct mail solicitations warning that "immediate action" was needed to save future Social Security and Medicare benefits. The organization now claims more than five million members.

NCPSSM has clearly benefited from modern computerized direct mail techniques, and more recently has increased the staff in its bright new office to forty-five—some of whom were hired away from government and from other organizations, including AARP. Having begun as a direct mail operation, NCPSSM gradually hired legislative staff persons and stepped up its lobbying on Capitol Hill (Fessler 1984). Its budget has swollen to thirty million, and it has the wealthiest political action committee of all old-age organizations. Like NASC, the other direct mail aging-based association, NCPSSM receives no government grants.

Among old-age membership groups with a more narrow occupational focus, the National Association of Retired Federal Employees is probably the most visible to national policy makers. NARFE was founded in 1921, around the time the Federal Employees Pension Act was passed, and now has a membership of about half a million—or one quarter of federal retirees and their survivors. The most aggressive recruiting is done out of the 1,700 local chapters; "that's where the action is," said a NARFE staffer.

NARFE's political activities have been confined mainly to bread-and-butter issues of concern to retired federal employees; involvement with the broader concerns of the other mass membership groups has been minimal. Still, because of the organization's longevity, its professional staff, and the political savvy of many members who are naturally familiar with federal public policy questions, NARFE maintains high visibility and respect among policy makers. Because of its narrow focus, NARFE maintains a legislative staff of only four, but it has a large political action committee and an annual budget of nearly five million dollars.

During the 1970s, in the wake of the 1971 White House Conference on Aging at which minority concerns became important topics of discussion, several groups were formed with a more narrowly defined policy focus. Working primarily on issues of concern to elderly blacks, Hispanics, native Americans, Asian Americans, and women, these groups consist mainly of policy professionals and academics. The Older Women's League (OWL) is somewhat of an exception in its membership composition; it is largely a grass-roots organization with more than ten thousand members and is loosely affiliated with the National Organization for Women. OWL was formed in 1980 by two Oakland, California women, Tish Sommers and Laurie Shields; its national headquarters is now in Washington D.C. OWL lobbies for legislation to end inequities for older working women; to improve women's benefits from pension plans, Social Security, and insurance policies; and to increase social services for older women.

The Villers Foundation was founded in 1980 and endowed with $40 million by philanthropists Philippe and Kate Villers, to work on public policy and legal assistance for the elderly poor. The organization's founders felt that existing groups were not focusing sufficiently on low-income elderly issues, and wished to fill the gap in the organizational landscape. Villers donates funds to individuals and groups—including other aging-based groups—for research and advocacy on these issues. It is not a membership organization, nor does it donate money to campaigns through a political action committee. It does, however, engage a small staff of well-connected lobbyists and policy specialists.

The National Council on the Aging is the largest of the organizations for professionals and service providers studying and serving the elderly. NCOA, a loose confederation of nearly seven thousand public and private social welfare agencies and specialists in gerontology and geriatrics, was founded in 1950, and serves as a center for information, planning, consulting, and publications in the aging field. NCOA maintains a large library and offices near Capitol Hill, with a staff of one hundred. Although less active politically than the mass membership organizations, NCOA's existence enhances the visibility and prestige of the gray lobby in Washington. Academic and medical organizations such as the Gerontological Society of America also add prominence to the political position of the elderly through expert research and occasional participation in hearings.[6]

What caused the explosion of aging-based organizations, and the mass membership groups in particular, during the last three decades?

[6] Most information on these organizations was drawn from Pratt (1976; 1983); Peirce and Choharis (1982); and Lammers (1983); as well as from my own interviews.

Scholars have attributed interest group origin and maintenance to at least four factors, and all have played a part in the growth of aging-based groups: (1) the growing sense of common needs and interests among older people, (2) the leadership of organizational "entrepreneurs," (3) the variety of incentives offered to members, and (4) patronage by government agencies and private foundations. However, it is the second and third of these factors—the interest group entrepreneurs and their array of membership incentives described in exchange theory—that have played the most prominent role.

The first factor—the increasing sense of common needs and problems—grew out of the earlier senior movement. Older people, as we have seen, began to mobilize around their common needs and interests during the early decades of the twentieth century. Technological and structural changes in the economy and in the family, and the economic hardships of the Great Depression, made older people receptive to the appeals of pension crusaders. These changes were disturbances of the type discussed by Truman (1971) and other interest group theorists: disruptive events that incite political action among relatively deprived groups (see also Freeman 1975).

The decade of the sixties was another frustrating time for large numbers of older people, particularly for the "downwardly mobile" elderly in the middle income range (Pratt 1976: 76–82; Nelson 1982). Inflation, including the rapidly rising cost of medical care, was hard on retired persons largely dependent on savings and fixed-income pensions in the days before Social Security cost-of-living adjustments and Medicare. Increased property taxes, deteriorating mass transit systems, lack of safe and decent housing for a growing elderly population, and nursing home abuses were all acute problems for many older people by the 1960s. The passage of Social Security had created rising expectations among older people that were not being adequately met. All of these changes increased the group-oriented feelings of relative deprivation among older people during the 1960s, in contrast with the more quiescent forties and fifties.

Older people, furthermore, are not politically passive. The "disengagement theory" advanced by many social scientists in mid-century— that the elderly tend to withdraw gradually from political and other prior activities—was largely discredited later by researchers studying political activity and controlling for such demographic variables as marital status, education, gender, and income. Most political activity, including voting, participating in election campaigns, and joining organizations, was found to remain stable or to increase beyond the age of sixty-five (S. Cutler 1977; Dobson 1983: 127–28; Nie et al. 1974;

Wolfinger and Rosenstone 1980). Education enhances political awareness and participation in all these activities, and the educational status
of older people is rising rapidly, both relatively and absolutely. The
educational disparity between young and old is diminishing, and may
even disappear by the time the baby boomers retire. The better health
and higher standard of living enjoyed by older people today, furthermore, are permitting more of them to engage in social and political
activities (Rose 1965a; Bengtson et al. 1985: 329; Williamson et al.
1982: 8).

In addition, several demographic trends of the past few decades have
increased interaction among older people while reducing some contact
between young and old. These include higher rates of voluntary retirement; self-segregating trends in migration, particularly to certain "Sun
Belt" states or to retirement communities; expansion of social welfare
services and facilities exclusively for seniors; and the decline in multigenerational households. The increased contact among older age
peers, researchers contend, had led to growing elderly group consciousness by the 1960s, with political activity a natural outgrowth of
this trend (Rose 1965b; Ragan and Dowd 1974).

The relationship between aging group consciousness and political
activity, however, is not so simple. Some people in the youth-oriented
culture of the twentieth century feel that old age is a negative referent;
the stigma attached to aging may lead to denial of personal old age and
discourage group solidarity (Beauvoir 1972; Fox 1981: 166). Empirical studies of group identification in the 1970s indicate that older people who name the elderly as the group they feel "closest to" tend to be
more female, less educated, and more likely to be retired than are older
people who identify primarily with other social groups (Dobson 1983:
135). Aging group consciousness was found to be negatively related to
political activity of various types, even after controlling for gender and
education (Dobson 1983: 137; Miller et al. 1981: 500–501).[7] On the
other hand, aging group consciousness coupled with faith in group ef-
ficacy—the belief that the group can do something to influence American politics—seems to promote, rather than retard, political participation (Miller et al. 1980).

Membership in senior organizations, further empirical study has
shown, is positively related both to aging group consciousness, as defined by seven questions on personal identification and political asso-

[7] Miller et al. (1981) use a definition of group consciousness that includes group identification, polar affect (differences in feelings toward groups), polar power (differences
in perceived influence of groups), and individual versus system blame for group problems.

ciation (Ward 1977), and to political group interest, or expressed willingness to advance the collective interests of older people (Trela 1972).
Does organization membership lead to greater political interest and
group solidarity, or is the reverse more often true? Direction of causal-
ity is difficult to determine in cross-sectional surveys, but the findings
noted on aging group consciousness indicate that most older people
need some type of inducement beyond group consciousness in order to
participate in political organizations for the elderly. During the last
two decades, organizational "entrepreneurs" have offered such in-
ducements in exchange for membership enrollment and participation,
thereby building up the stability and organizational surpluses necessary for ongoing political advocacy (Salisbury 1969; Wilson 1973;
Weissman 1970). This type of entrepreneurial exchange has helped
create the large and diverse senior organizations thriving today.

The leaders of the modern senior political organizations, unlike the
personalistic, dominant leaders of the earlier groups, have been more
low-key, functioning behind the scenes in almost business managerial
style (Pratt 1976: 51). The Gray Panthers' Maggie Kuhn is the major
exception, but the Panthers, too, have adopted a somewhat more formal and hierarchical leadership structure since the late 1970s (Jacobs
1980). All of the leaders of the mass membership senior groups have
built and sustained their memberships by offering some combination
of material, solidary, and purposive incentives. Both AARP and NCSC
boast millions of members largely because of the material benefits and
services that supplement their political, or purposive, appeals. The
Gray Panthers have relied much more on purposive incentives to maintain a smaller but politically active membership. All three, in addition,
have offered solidary incentives by organizing thousands of local chapters and clubs. Pratt (1983: 151–52) has attributed much of their stability and recruitment success to the existence of these local clubs.

The two newer mass membership organizations, NASC and NCPSSM,
in contrast, have bypassed local organization and, as noted earlier,
have relied instead on computerized mass mailings for membership recruitment. NASC and, to a lesser extent, NCPSSM both offer material
benefits to their members. In addition, both offer a type of purposive
incentive that has become quite common with the widespread use of
computerized mass mailings: a form letter with an urgent appeal for
the support of some political goal, such as "saving" a Social Security
trust fund facing imminent financial "crisis." For the price of a set
membership fee or donation, the donor receives a membership card
and the satisfaction of supporting a worthy cause. The satisfaction of

such "checkbook affiliation" may be momentary, but the cost in terms of time commitment is low (Hayes 1983).

Finally, modern aging-based organizations have benefited from the expansion of the "aging enterprise": "the congeries of programs, organizations, bureaucracies, interest groups, trade associations, providers, industries, and professionals that serve the aged in one capacity or another" (Estes 1979: 2). The interest groups and other elements of the aging enterprise provide a good deal of mutual support. Interest group advocacy keeps pressure on the government to continue funding aging-based agencies and research. The interest groups receive, in turn, financial and organizational resources for their own work. The patronage of government agencies and private foundations and associations that serve the elderly has propelled the growth and politicization of existing interest groups and the emergence of new ones (Walker 1983; Vinyard 1978; Pratt 1976: 41; Cutler 1981: 153).

The result of all of this organizational growth and activity during the past two or three decades is that policy makers now see older people as a formidable political force in their own right. Organizations of older people were, by most accounts, secondary actors in the struggle for Social Security, Medicare, and other political gains for the elderly during the first three-fourths of the twentieth century. They are now, according to many written accounts as well as to most of my interviews with government officials and employees, their own best and most visible advocates. Many observers agree with John F. Cogan of Stanford University's Hoover Institution that "the clear winner" in the wake of the 1980s federal budget cutbacks "has been the elderly. . . . They've escaped every attempt at retrenchment" (quoted in Rauch 1987: 126).

CONCLUSION

The aging political movement clearly has reached the institutional phase of development, marked by long-lived organizations with established memberships, substantial resources, leadership stability and succession, hierarchical structure, and government connections. Aging-based interest groups are at the pinnacle of their organizational success and have achieved Washington insider status.

Coalition building, both among old-age organizations and between elderly and nonelderly groups, has been important to senior advocacy, but the importance has varied over time. Older people, we have noted before, are a diverse lot, and their heterogeneity is reflected in the variety of organizations claiming to represent them. But the diversity of organizations has not prevented them from working together. As Freeman (1975: 151) has observed, "American movements have thrived best when they were highly pluralistic, with each group within them having a solid identity and sense of purpose rather than trying to be everything to everyone." Collaborative effort among the senior organizations has become more common during the late 1970s and 1980s, as the groups have stabilized and matured, and as each group's individual identity has solidified. The Leadership Council of Aging Organizations, founded in 1978, is the most prominent example; it helped unify the groups' fight against the Reagan administration's proposed Social Security cutbacks (Pratt 1982: 32), and it still exists as a coalition today.

Old-age groups have also formed coalitions frequently with nonelderly groups. Shifting coalitions organized temporarily around single issues are more prevalent than ever today, as policy networks have become more permeable and the number of single-issue and other interest groups has grown (Gais et al. 1984; Light 1985: 81; Salisbury 1983: 368). Williamson, Evans, and Powell, arguing that old-age political activity fits their "coalition formation" model, observe that "old-age policy gains have typically occurred when the aging lobby has had the strong backing of other interest groups" (1982: 12). During the 1960s and early 1970s, for example, the support of organized labor was critical to the passage of Medicare and improvements in Social Security; the blind and disabled helped work for expanded Supplemental Security Income benefits; consumer groups pressed for regulation of nursing homes and prescription drugs; social welfare lobbies aided the elderly on a number of issues. These groups themselves have benefited from their association with the elderly, because of elite and general public veneration of older people as a "deserving needy" group (Elder and Cobb 1984: 119; Lammers 1983: 64; Vinyard 1978: 25).

However, as we shall see in chapter 5, the old-age organizations eventually became a formidable political force in their own right, less dependent upon coalition partners. Today, aging-based organizations are more often senior partners in these coalitions, rather than the peripheral actors that they were prior to the mid-1970s. Many consider the old-age groups to be among "the most potent lobbyists on human services issues" (Peirce and Choharis 1982: 1560). In fact, the larger and more self-sufficient aging-based organizations—especially AARP—have become more cautious about coalition building, hesitating to lend their names to certain causes or to share credit if there is no need to pool resources with others.

At least one recent development is likely to push old-age groups into continuing their coalition building with nonelderly groups. In 1976,

Pratt wrote that "the elderly constitute an 'unrivaled minority,' a politicized group which has no institutionalized and self-proclaimed political adversaries" (p. 83). But this, too, is changing. There is growing evidence of a backlash among policy elites against the policy gains of the elderly (see, e.g., Hudson 1978; Samuelson 1981; Longman 1985). A new group, Americans for Generational Equity (AGE), founded by Paul Hewitt—a former aide to Republican Senator Dave Durenberger—and backed by corporate donors, warns that Social Security may soon collapse unless benefits are means-tested or taxed at high income levels, the federal budget is balanced, and tax incentives for private retirement plans are increased. The response of old-age organizations has been involvement in Generations United, a new coalition of groups representing children and the elderly. The National Council on the Aging and the Child Welfare League, along with over one hundred other groups, formed Generations United to counter the charge that older people are benefiting at the expense of younger age groups.

How serious is the backlash against the elderly, and how will it affect aging-based interest groups in the near future? We will explore these questions further in the following chapters, covering public opinion toward old-age benefits, organizational recruitment and representation of older people, and the role of old-age organizations in the national aging policy process.

CHAPTER 3

Political Attitudes of the Elderly

OLDER Americans share some common political concerns; as a group, they benefit from a broad range of government policies and programs. At the same time, older people are highly diverse, ranging widely in social status, health, income, education, style and quality of life, and often maintaining group identities and memberships forged earlier in life. How cohesive are older people in their political attitudes and opinions, and how salient are the issues that affect the elderly as a group? If older people are divided on these issues, who among them supports increased government benefits for the elderly, and who does not?

Older people, according to the evidence presented in this chapter, are deeply divided on aging policy issues, particularly along economic and partisan lines. Collectively, they are no more supportive of government benefits for the elderly than are younger adults. Thus, these findings contradict the idea that older people's political attitudes are group-interest based. They also dispute the notion that aging policy is fraught with conflict between the generations.

Previous findings about elderly group cohesion on a number of issues—including aging policy issues—have been inconclusive and often contradictory. These earlier studies often suffered from the lack of specific questions on aging policy and from small numbers of elderly respondents, but more recent data have corrected these inadequacies. This chapter is a summary and an update of previous findings. The update, using survey data from the 1970s and early 1980s,[1] has two purposes. The first is to test for attitudinal differences between older and younger adults in several policy areas, particularly those areas which affect the elderly most directly. The second purpose is to exam-

[1] The data used in this chapter were made available by the Inter-University Consortium for Political and Social Research, through the State Data Program at the University of California. The data were originally collected by the Center for Political Studies of the Institute for Social Research, the University of Michigan, for the National Election Studies; by James A. Davis, Tom W. Smith, and the National Opinion Research Center, University of Chicago, for the National Data Program for the Social Sciences; and by ABC News and the *Washington Post*. Neither the collectors nor the distributors of the data bear any responsibility for the analyses or interpretations presented here.

ine the sources of agreement and divergence among older people to see how they differ along social, economic, and partisan lines.

The chapter begins with a review of group-related concepts used in survey data analysis. A review of concepts and findings from previous studies of older Americans' political attitudes follows. Finally, I present the findings from my own analysis.

GROUP INFLUENCE ON INDIVIDUAL POLICY PREFERENCES

Theories about the influence of groups on political attitudes have become increasingly complex since the advent of survey data analysis. Group-based studies have focused on racial, ethnic, social class, gender, religious, occupational, age, and many other categories of people. The focus of these studies has expanded from demographic characteristics to include psychological group identification as well (Rhodebeck 1985). Groups may structure an individual's political attitudes and priorities by virtue of his membership in, feelings toward, and/or psychological attachment to them. While the identification of group-based attitudes may not be analytically straightforward, there is evidence that people do distinguish between personal, group, and national interests (e.g., Kinder et al. 1985).

Group-related issues may have political significance for a group member even if her personal life remains unaffected by those issues (Conover 1985: 764). An older homeowner, for example, may favor housing subsidies for the elderly out of affinity with her age group, not because she lacks housing herself. Group effects on attitudes often transcend or contradict partisan and ideological (liberal/conservative) preferences. Group influences are strongest on issues that are narrowly group-related, while ideological and partisan ties help shape attitudes on a broader range of policy areas (Rhodebeck 1985: 14). Our elderly homeowner, for example, might favor higher government spending on a variety of programs directly benefiting older people—including Social Security, Medicare, and funding for senior centers—while taking a more conservative position toward everything else from foreign aid to public education.

Several familiar concepts have emerged from the group literature to put these distinctions into theoretical perspective and to help explain the various ways in which groups structure political attitudes. Group *membership* refers to the objective characteristics linking a person to a group—in the case of the elderly, chronological age.[2] Group *identification* refers to a subjective attachment or closeness to a group in addition to membership (Conover 1985, 1984). Empirically, it is often measured with the use of survey questions on respondents' "feelings of closeness" to particular groups.[3]

Group *consciousness* refers to a more politicized awareness of interests that are shared by the members of a group and addressed through group political activity (Miller et al. 1981; Conover 1985; Ragan and Dowd 1974: 139). The definition of group consciousness lacks precision, but it generally contains some or all of the following elements: group membership and identification, perceived interdependence between one's own interests and those of the group, feelings of deprivation or worthiness relative to other groups in society, and commitment to political action on behalf of fellow group members. These are manifested in expressed attitudes and policy positions as well as in political activities such as voting, participation in campaigns, organizational memberships, and letter writing or other pressure tactics.

To assess the importance and pervasiveness of group influence upon older people's political attitudes, I will examine the effects of elderly group membership and identification on various policy preferences and priorities. If group consciousness is strong among the elderly, they should show a high degree of approval of and attention to policies directly affecting most older people. Such cohesion does not necessarily lead to a commitment to political action, but it is a start.

THE POLITICAL SALIENCE OF OLD AGE

How instrumental is old age in shaping political opinions? Even if we can establish that groups in general play a significant role in structuring political attitudes, is there a basis for claiming that old age in particular plays such a role? Suppose our elderly homeowner is also a woman, a Catholic, and a retired teacher: might she identify more closely in her political views with other women, Catholics, teachers, or homeowners, than with those in her age group? Alternatively, are her

---

[2] I use this definition of "membership" in this chapter to conform with the general usage of the term in survey data analysis. Elsewhere in this book, "membership" refers to members of a particular organization.

[3] While the prevailing definition of group identification contains both elements—membership and psychological attachment—some feel that the membership requirement is limiting, and that the key influences are psychological (e.g., Rhodebeck 1985: 3). Here I will look at the effects of psychological attachment to older people on all age groups, but the emphasis remains on those sixty-five years of age and over.

other group identities—gender and retirement status, for example—likely to reinforce her political identification with older people? Researchers are divided on this question of aging group consciousness.

There are, first, several contemporary conditions likely to enhance the relevance of old age to political attitudes. Today's older generation has witnessed the birth and growth of many old-age government benefits; tomorrow's elderly will have been socialized in a world in which such benefits always existed. Their old age may therefore be more politically relevant than ever before (Cutler 1981: 151). Political mobilization around the defense of programs that already exist is generally easier, more clearly focused, and less costly than collective action to attain new benefits (Hardin 1982: 62–64). In this context, aging-based organizations have expanded in number and size, and now enjoy a good deal of legitimacy and respect among policy makers. These organizations have both profited from and contributed to the rise of aging group consciousness (see, e.g., Pratt 1976, 1983; Cutler 1981). In addition, political party attachments appear to be on the decline, so that current and future generations are more likely to organize their political attitudes along group rather than partisan lines (Cutler 1981).

Not only do the elderly have a stake in the system, following the passage of so much favorable legislation during the past few decades, but now that stake is in jeopardy. Federal deficits and a sluggish economy are threatening the viability of Social Security, Medicare, and other programs benefiting the elderly. These threats are not just an outcome of retrenchment and Reaganism in the 1980s; they are likely to remain as the older population grows in relation to other age groups. One result may be political backlash against old-age programs; some opposition is evident already among journalists and politicians (Binstock 1983; Hudson 1978). Another result may be increased group consciousness, as political appeals to group members seem to be more effective when groups are threatened (Hansen 1985: 92).

Age group differentiation and stereotyping may accompany such current trends as earlier retirement, senior migration to the Sun Belt, and expanding services and facilities for the elderly exclusively. These trends often isolate the elderly from younger people (Bengtson et al. 1985: 329; Williamson et al. 1982: 8). This can also add to older people's feelings of age consciousness and political relevance as a group.

On the other hand, growing age segregation could inhibit group consciousness by stigmatizing old age and leading older people to disavow their common interests (Fox 1981). It is also possible that aging political consciousness—what there was of it—has already peaked and is in decline, now that the elderly have achieved so many political benefits and are better off financially. Perhaps now they can "afford" to be complacent—as long as they perceive no threats to their political gains. Indeed, there is evidence of political apathy even among rank-and-file members of the aging-based organizations (Pratt 1983: 169).

Given this wide range of scholarly opinion, it is hard to predict to what extent old age will be a significant basis for political attitudes and priorities. The same can probably be said about any group in a complex society. With the elderly, there is an additional complication, assuming that age group differences are found in the first place. Variations in policy preferences among older people may be the result of three different effects: maturation, cohort, and period. Maturation effects are those based on the universal process of aging; cohort effects are those based on the particular experiences of an age cohort as it moves through the life cycle; period effects are those that affect all age groups at a particular point in time. To separate these three types of effects requires a combination of longitudinal survey analysis and certain theoretical assumptions or interpretations (Riley 1973; Bengtson et al. 1985).

Maturation effects arise from the commonality of interests among older people at any point in history—interests or problems that arise as a result of the aging process. Health policy is an example of an issue that has shown age differences based on maturation effects, since health problems frequently accompany old age (Bengtson et al. 1985: 32). Issues relating to retirement also become more important as people reach a specified chronological age.

Cohort effects reflect the socialization of persons who were born around the same time and experienced the same set of unique historical circumstances. The cohort that will reach retirement age at the beginning of the twenty-first century, for example, was born around the time that Social Security was first enacted, and entered young adulthood during the debates over enactment of Medicare. Its members are thus more likely to take these programs for granted once they reach the age of eligibility (Cutler 1981: 151). Similarly, today's older people are less inclined than the young to favor certain social changes, such as legalization of abortion, not because they are closed-minded or conservative, but because such changes were not on the political agenda for many of their adult years (Hudson and Strate 1985: 561).

Period effects arise from historical trends or events that appear to change the opinions of persons in all age groups in the same direction. Support for Social Security and Medicare has, for example, been popular with adults of all ages. Support may wax and wane a bit over the years, but there is little indication of age group conflict over such issues (National Council on the Aging 1981; Shapiro and Smith 1985). Changes in political priorities offer another example. The National Election Studies have asked every two years since 1960, "What do you think are the most important problems facing the country?" There have been broad shifts over the years between foreign policy and the domestic economy as the most important problem, but these shifts have occurred simultaneously among all age groups (Campbell and Strate 1981: 587–89).

It is important to distinguish among these three types of effects, in studying the nature and degree of political discord between age groups. It is difficult, however, to find data that are ideal for the type of analysis—referred to as "cohort analysis"—that will most effectively separate these three effects and their combinations or interactions. This type of analysis requires survey questions that are asked repeatedly, without changes in question wording, over a period of many years; panel data are of course even better. This chapter does not include a formal cohort analysis, due to the lack of available data. The omission, however, turns out to be unimportant. Cohort analysis is most valuable for the study of discord between age groups; and the data analyzed in this chapter show very little divergence between older and younger adults. Instead, the differences among older people are sharper and more interesting than differences between the old and the young. Data from several recent surveys dealing with policy opinions and priorities are examined for evidence of age-group differences, elderly cohesion, and old-age organizational potential, following a summary of previous findings from earlier data analyses.

Previous Findings on Older People's Political Attitudes

Age-group analyses of political attitudes have used survey data stretching across three decades—the 1950s through the 1970s. Perhaps the central question about older people's policy positions until the early 1970s was: "Are they more conservative than younger people?" By the mid-seventies, the central question had become: "Do their policy positions reflect group-oriented interests?" But whatever the focus, past empirical evidence was seldom conclusive. Sometimes older people appeared to be somewhat more conservative, other times more liberal. Sometimes there appeared to be little or no difference in policy positions across age groups; other times there appeared to be significant differences between people over and under the age of sixty-five.

Many of these studies indicated that older Americans, while showing little ideological consistency across issues, tended to be more favorable toward policies of particular importance to the elderly, both compared to other age groups and relative to other types of issues. No one found a great deal of consistency within, or polarization between, age groups; no one predicted widespread intergenerational conflict; but evidence of elderly group interest was significant. Older people were generally more conservative on social issues such as abortion, pollution, legalization of marijuana, and women's roles, as well as on questions about civil rights and law and order. Their foreign policy opinions tended to be more isolationist. Their positions on domestic economic policy were more mixed, but tended to fall along group-interest lines. Older people were, for example, more favorable toward government spending on health care, less concerned about rising taxes, and more opposed to spending on education (Campbell 1971: 114–15; Campbell and Strate 1981: 583–87; Hudson and Strate 1985: 560–62).

Health policy is the issue that has most often been studied in relation to policy positions of the elderly, for two reasons: it has particular relevance to older people, who tend to have more health problems, and the issue has appeared frequently in social surveys. (Questions on other aging policies, such as Social Security, Medicare, and old-age social services, were rare before the 1980s.) Responding to questions about whether the government should provide medical aid or medical insurance, the sixty-five-and-over age group has seemed to be consistently favorable, both absolutely and compared to other age groups (Bengtson et al. 1985: 311–13; Weaver 1976; Schreiber and Marsden 1972).

Not all studies of issue opinions, however, have concluded that older people tend to favor old-age government benefits. One study found no difference between old and young persons on a generalized measure of support for old-age benefits (Dobson and St. Angelo 1980); another, conducted in Alabama, found even less support among persons sixty and over for the use of age as a criterion for service and benefit eligibility, compared to younger respondents (Klemmack and Roff 1980: 151). A recent Gallup poll showed virtually no age difference in opinions toward cutting " 'entitlement' programs such as Social Security, Medicare, and the like" in order to reduce the federal deficit; nearly everyone in every age group was against such cuts (Gallup Report 1985). Finally, a study of survey responses to hypothetical depictions of older people and children in poverty showed older people divided along income lines, rather than united in support of benefits to the elderly poor (Ponza et al. 1988). These results suggest that either the elderly do not base their policy positions to a great extent on group interest, or they base their positions on the interests of other, non-age-based groups—or both.

On the health issue, an analysis of questions on federal spending on various programs found the elderly to be less supportive of national health care programs than were other age groups (Clemente 1975: 62). Furthermore, among studies already cited, the results varied when controlled for several socioeconomic characteristics such as education and income. One study found that standardizing such variables made no difference (Weaver 1976: 614), while another found that controlling for income and occupation made the relationship between age and support for government health benefits decline or even disappear (Schreiber and Marsden 1972).

There is in fact little conflict between age groups over support for government benefits for the elderly. Whether asked about specific aging-based policies, or asked to compare the elderly with other groups as potential government beneficiaries, people of all ages have overwhelmingly, and over several decades, voiced approval of old-age benefits, giving the elderly a special political legitimacy in the eyes of the public (Hudson and Strate 1985: 571; Klemmack and Roff 1980: 149). However, if older people diverge little from younger people in many policy positions, perhaps they are distinct in the salience they attribute to issues that directly affect them. What *is* important to older people?

The problems that concern the elderly in their personal lives are, apparently, not much different from those that plague their younger peers. In a 1981 poll conducted by Louis Harris and Associates for the National Council on the Aging, the "high cost of energy" topped the list of ten "very serious" problems for adults both older and younger than sixty-five years. "Fear of crime" and "not having enough money to live on" also ranked high among both groups in 1981 and in a similar poll conducted in 1974. The differences that did exist between the over- and under-sixty-five age groups were not large; the biggest difference was in "poor health," cited as a very serious problem by 21 percent of the older group and only nine percent of the younger group (National Council on the Aging 1981: 5–7).

None of the ten problems was cited as very serious by a majority of older people. Both old and young, however, greatly overestimated the seriousness of all ten problems "for most people over 65," and many older people seemed to think they were unusually problem-free among their age peers (National Council on the Aging 1981: 8–10; O'Gorman 1980). The personal problems of older people, then, may not be serious enough, in the aggregate, to promote mass political activity by the elderly; and even if they were, personal problems are seldom politicized in the United States (Brody and Sniderman 1977). However, there does seem to be a great deal of concern for the elderly as a group. Are these concerns reflected in political attitudes and in perceptions of major national problems?

The literature on age and policy priorities is less extensive than that on issue positions, but here, differences by age seem even less evident. An analysis of the "most important national problems" mentioned by American National Election Study respondents between 1960 and 1980 revealed negligible age differences, and almost no one of any age mentioned problems specific to the elderly, such as Social Security or Medicare. The small differences between age groups were "quite overshadowed by the massive period effects—reactions to conditions of the time" (Campbell and Strate 1981: 588). Similar findings—that is, evidence of period effects but no differences across age groups—emerged from a study of Gallup Poll data from 1940 through 1970 on perceived national and community problems (Douglass et al. 1974). A 1982 survey of elderly voters in the North Dakota Silver-Haired Legislative election,[4] on the other hand, revealed a high degree of cohesion around the prominence of four aging-related issues (Smith and Martinson 1984). While this survey was surely affected by the context—an election that naturally draws special attention to aging policy—it may also be indicative of the potential, in the 1980s, for increased aging group consciousness.

Diversity among older people can help explain their lack of cohesion on political priorities. Where are the political cleavages among the elderly? What types of older people are more likely to support aging-based programs and benefits? If there is potential for heightened group consciousness and political activity among the elderly, where does this potential show the most promise?

Many researchers on the politics of aging recognize, and often control for, various demographic and socioeconomic characteristics—particularly education and gender, since the elderly have been disproportionately female and less educated. However, few have comprehensively examined the differential effects of these variables on older people's political attitudes. Probably the most work in this area has been in studies of political participation. Some researchers have found, for

[4] "Silver-haired" or "senior" legislatures, active now in more than twenty states, are composed of senior citizens elected by older people in their states to hold mock legislatures, set aging policy priorities, draft "bills" encompassing those priorities, and then lobby the real state legislature to pass those measures into law.

example, that when controlling for such variables, political participation in various forms does not drop off after the age of sixty-five; in fact, it often increases (e.g., Verba and Nie 1972: 138–48; Wolfinger and Rosenstone 1980: 46–50). Studies of policy positions that control for such variables have often contradicted each other, as we saw in the studies of health policy opinions cited earlier.

Subjective old age—feelings of closeness to, or identification with, older people as a group—may also be related to political attitudes, perhaps more so than simple chronological age. The vast literature on the effects of group identification upon attitudes includes some references to the elderly in particular. Older people who say they feel "closest to" the elderly as a group, for example, have been found to be more liberal on economic or government spending issues, and more conservative on social issues such as abortion and pollution (Cutler and Schmidhauser 1975: 389–90; Conover 1984: 779). In a similar vein, other researchers have found that older people who are members of aging-based organizations are more likely to have "more demands, resentments, and pride associated with aging" (Rose 1965a: 29–34), and to have "strong feelings of activist self-interest" based on their age (Trela 1972: 246–47). At the same time, however, aging group identification—feeling "closest to" older people—appears to be negatively correlated with many forms of political participation, including voting, attempting to influence others, working in campaigns, and writing to public officials. This relationship may be due largely to the socioeconomic characteristics of old-age group identifiers; they do tend to be female, retired, and less educated (Dobson 1983: 135–38; Miller et al. 1980: 693–99).

Previous findings on the political priorities of older Americans, to sum up, have proved largely inconclusive, and so, therefore, have their implications for the political mobilization of the elderly. There is some evidence of a slight group-benefits orientation and an emerging group consciousness among older people, however, and only an update of previous research will reveal whether these trends are continuing. While there may not be a monolithic movement of older people on the horizon, it is possible that they will increasingly place demands on government to meet their age-related needs. Already their organizations are thriving, nationally and locally. They are a group worth watching.

What are the policy priorities of older Americans in the 1980s? In the context of the federal deficit crisis, the increased media attention to Social Security and Medicare costs, the courting of the elderly vote by both parties, and the early signs of a political backlash against current spending levels on the aging, will cohesion on policy positions among the elderly, and the importance of aging policy issues, increase? Or is old age relatively unimportant as a political referent? What types of factors would be likely to increase the potential for group cohesion, and what types of older people are most likely to support increases in old-age benefits? These are the major questions addressed in this chapter.

THE DATA

The objectives of the data analysis to follow are:

1. to update previous work on the policy positions of older people, using data from the first half of the 1980s and concentrating in particular on aging-related issues such as Social Security, health care policy, and mandatory retirement;
2. to see if aging-related problems are beginning to emerge among the answers to questions about the "most important national problems";
3. to examine the effects of selected demographic and socioeconomic variables upon the relationships (or nonrelationships, as the case may be) between age and political attitudes;
4. to see if elderly group identification has increased among older people, and to look at its effects upon their issue positions; and
5. to examine the relationships between older people's policy positions and their assessments of the national economy, the economic situation of the elderly as a group, and their own personal financial situation.

A few recent public opinion surveys have focused on the politics of old age, paralleling the heightened attention to aging-related issues by politicians and the media. Three different data sources are used in this analysis.

The American National Election Studies (hereafter referred to as NES) have been conducted by the Center for Political Studies, University of Michigan, every two years since 1952. Their extensive questions on a variety of political topics have served as the basis for many of the studies cited earlier, especially the questions on specific policy positions and important national problems. In 1982, 1984, and 1986 there were also questions about federal spending in several policy areas—among them, Social Security and Medicare—asking respondents whether spending in these areas should be increased, decreased, or left at current levels. These questions are useful because of the variety of policy areas covered in the same question format, thus offering some idea of which programs are relatively more or less important to respondents.

The General Social Surveys (GSS), conducted most years by the National Opinion Research Center since 1972, were also used in some of the studies cited earliier, and also cover a broad range of social and political topics. The GSS has asked questions about federal spending levels in specific policy areas since 1973 (although Social Security questions did not appear until 1984), allowing comparisons over time.

Finally, the ABC News/*Washington Post* Poll of Public Opinion on Aging (1982) contains questions on aging policy and the national economy, as well as questions about respondents' personal problems and financial situation. This poll includes an oversample of elderly persons, providing an exceptional opportunity to examine the sources of contention and agreement among older people around aging policy issues.

In the analyses to follow, respondents are divided into three age groups: older people, sixty-five years and over; middle-aged people, thirty-six to sixty-four years; and young adults, eighteen to thirty-five years. While no chronological division is perfect for defining "the elderly," sixty-five marks the age at which working people are eligible for full retirement benefits, and it is therefore the most natural cutoff point for purposes of comparison. The relevant comparisons are between older people on the one hand, and the two younger groups on the other. Differences between the middle-aged and the young are rarely discussed here, except when the older group is very similar to one while very different from the other.

FINDINGS: COMPARISONS ACROSS AGE GROUPS

The first set of findings comes as something of a surprise. Older people are nearly indistinguishable from younger adults on most issues—including aging policy issues. In fact, by some measures they seem even *less* supportive of government benefits for the elderly than are middle-aged and young adults. If older people, in the political context of the 1980s, have increased their group consciousness around substantive issues, it is not evident in the data analyzed here.

The General Social Survey questions about federal spending—whether it is "too much," "too little," or "about the right amount"—have covered many policy areas, including social welfare (health, welfare, education, blacks, Social Security), social control (crime, drugs), local improvements (cities, mass transportation, parks and recreation), foreign relations (defense, foreign aid), space exploration, and the environment. A comparison of age group differences at four points in time that span more than a decade—1974, 1980, 1984, and 1986—finds almost no change in the degree and direction of age difference. The only area in which older people seemed to favor more spending than the younger groups was national defense, and that difference disappeared in 1984. While the differences on other issues were not large, older people tended to be less supportive of federal spending on space exploration, the environment, cities, blacks, parks, and (not surprisingly) education, as well as (surprisingly) health in 1974 and 1980, and Social Security in 1984 and 1986.

NES data in 1982, 1984, and 1986 produced similar results for the questions about federal spending. In 1984, for example, older people did not differ from the other age groups by more than a few percentage points in their opinions toward spending on Social Security, Medicare, science, the environment, crime, national defense, jobs, blacks, and food stamps. The only policy area with a sizable age difference was the public school system; 64 percent of the young, and 49 percent of the middle-aged, said that spending on schools should be increased, while only 43 percent of those sixty-five and over agreed.

The 1984 distribution of responses for the two programs most relevant to the aging—Social Security and Medicare—appears in Table 1.

Table 1. Opinions Toward Federal Spending on Social Security and Medicare, 1984 (Percent)

	Age		
	18 to 35	36 to 64	65 and over
Social Security			
Increase	55	53	45
Same	41	44	53
Decrease	5	4	1
N	766	804	309
Medicare			
Increase	51	50	47
Same	43	46	50
Decrease	6	5	2
N	767	796	302

Source: American National Election Study, 1984. See appendix for exact question wording.

Almost no one favored a decrease in federal spending on Social Security, as is well known. But even in 1984, on the heels of the much-publicized crisis in the Social Security trust fund, the elderly were less likely than the other two age groups to favor increases in Social Security; the majority of older people were satisfied with spending at its current level. The results were the same, though less pronounced, for Medicare.

Nor are older people in the 1980s very distinct from other age groups in their opinions toward government-funded medical insurance. Earlier analyses, as noted above, had found older people to be consistently more favorable toward federal medical assistance, usually by ten to fifteen percentage points (Weaver 1976; Schreiber and Marsden 1972; Bengtson et al. 1985: 312). These analyses all ended with 1968 or 1972 data. In 1976, 1980, and 1984, the NES again asked respondents whether they thought medical insurance should be funded by the government, or by private individuals and companies. The 1978 results were similar to earlier years, as can be seen in Table 2; older people were again more likely than the others to choose government as the provider. However, in 1976, and again in 1984, the difference between the three age groups had diminished. In fact, what stands out most in Table 2 for all three years—1976, 1978, and 1984—is the division *within* age groups, not between them. Government funded medical insurance apparently is a controversial issue among people of all ages, and not one that tends to unite older people against the middle-aged and the young.

Finally, when ABC News and the *Washington Post* asked respondents in 1982 whether they felt the U.S. government was spending "as much as it should on the elderly, more than it should or not as much as it should," the youngest age group came out most in favor of increasing federal spending on the elderly; the middle-aged group also resoundingly supported increased spending; and the elderly themselves supported more spending by a bare majority of 51 percent. Furthermore, although very few people favored reduced spending on the elderly, a higher percentage of older people chose this alternative, as can be seen in Table 3. Clearly the older population was not acting like a proper "special interest group."

When asked on the same survey whether there were any circumstances under which Medicare should be cut back, respondents of all ages were almost equally opposed to Medicare cutbacks, as seen in Table 4. Opposition was overwhelming, despite question wording suggesting that there is a "financial crunch" and that "other government programs" are facing the budgetary axe. Thus Medicare, in contrast to

Table 2. Opinions Toward Government Funded vs. Privately Funded Medical Insurance, 1976, 1978, 1984 (Percent)

	Age		
	18 to 35	*36 to 64*	*65 and over*
1976			
Government	46	40	46
Neither	11	13	17
Private	43	47	37
N	*676*	*789*	*304*
1978			
Government	43	43	57
Neither	14	13	10
Private	43	44	32
N	*800*	*825*	*259*
1984			
Government	39	35	40
Neither	17	23	23
Private	44	42	36
N	*306*	*341*	*141*

Source: American National Election Study, 1976, 1978, and 1984. See appendix for exact question wording.

Note: Respondents were asked to place themselves on a 7-point scale. "Government" refers to points 1-3. "Neither" refers to point 4; "Private" refers to points 5-7.

Table 3. Opinions Toward U.S. Government Spending on the Elderly, 1982 (Percent)

	Age		
	18 to 35	*36 to 64*	*65 and over*
Government . . .			
Spends not enough	78	67	51
Spends enough	18	26	40
Spends too much	4	7	9
weighted N	*684*	*667*	*231*

Source: ABC News/*Washington Post* Poll of Public Opinion on Aging. See appendix for exact question wording.

Note: Numbers are weighted to correct for the elderly oversample.

Table 4. Opinions Toward Cutbacks in Medicare, 1982 (Percent)

	Age		
	18 to 35	*36 to 64*	*65 and over*
Never cut	87	85	89
Cut back	13	15	11
weighted N	684	667	231

Source: ABC News/*Washington Post* Poll of Public Opinion on Aging, 1982. See appendix for exact question wording.
Note: Numbers are weighted to correct for the elderly oversample.

Table 5. Opinions Toward Mandatory Retirement, 1982 (Percent)

	Age		
	18 to 35	*36 to 64*	*65 and over*
Favor	23	30	32
Oppose	77	70	68
weighted N	707	681	238

Source: ABC News/*Washington Post* Poll of Public Opinion on Aging, 1982. See appendix for exact question wording.
Note: Numbers are weighted to correct for the elderly oversample.

government-funded medical insurance in general, seems to be extremely popular. But like the medical insurance issue, it is not one that shows any sign of pitting old against young.

Another issue covered in the ABC News/*Washington Post* poll was that of mandatory retirement. When Congress abolished mandatory retirement prior to age seventy in 1978, and abolished it altogether in 1986, it was considered a victory for older people, who had allegedly been victims of age discrimination. The largest aging-based organization, the American Association of Retired Persons, among other groups, had lobbied hard against mandatory retirement (Pratt 1983: 157–58). Their advocacy was enhanced considerably within Congress by the leadership of Democratic Representative Claude Pepper of Florida, a major champion of old-age benefits and elimination of age discrimination. Responses to the question in 1982 indicated that, indeed, majorities of all ages did oppose mandatory retirement. Older people, however, opposed it the *least* (see Table 5).

Older people in the first half of the 1980s, it seems, were not very distinctive in their positions on aging policy issues. But what about their opinions on the importance of these issues? Are older people beginning to view aging-related issues as among the most important in national politics? Apparently not. An examination of responses to the 1984 NES question, "What do you think are the most important problems facing this country?" reveals findings similar to those of Campbell and Strate (1981: 587–90), who looked at the data for 1960–1980. The older and younger groups are nearly identical in their responses; all three groups are quite evenly divided in 1984 between the economy and foreign policy/defense issues as the modal categories. The number of people mentioning specifically aging-related issues as one of the three major problems does not surpass 8 percent (for the middle-aged group); for the young, it is 6 percent; for the elderly, it is 5 percent.

Older Americans seem to be as divided as their younger peers over questions on political issues and priorities—even those that affect them most directly. What are the bases of those divisions among the elderly? In the following sections, four possible types of factors are explored, using recent survey data: demographic and socioeconomic variables; group identification or psychological closeness to the elderly; economic outlook for the elderly as a group and the nation as a whole; and personal problems, financial situation, and sources of income.

Demographic and Socioeconomic Variables

Studies abound of the relationships between political attitudes and personal characteristics—such as race, sex, income, education, occupation, social class, and region. It is well known that people at the lower end of the socioeconomic scale, or members of disadvantaged groups—for example, those who are nonwhite, poor, working-class, or uneducated—tend to express more liberal positions on social welfare issues. Likewise, Democrats and self-proclaimed liberals tend to favor more federal domestic spending than do Republicans and conservatives. The findings on aging policy issues are, in general, the same. In studying the relationship between personal characteristics and aging policy positions, we are looking for two things in particular: variables that change the nature of relationships between age and political attitudes when held constant, and variables that show the deepest divisions among older people. The results of such an analysis, coupled with demographic projections of the future elderly population, can help predict, however tenuously, the pattern of older people's attitudes in the years to come.

Respondents of all ages diverged in predictable ways in their attitudes toward Social Security and Medicare; the NES data showed divisions by income, race, education, subjective social class, political party, and ideology.[5] Pluralities of people who were low-income, nonwhite, less educated, working-class, Democratic, or liberal favored increases in Social Security and Medicare, while pluralities of higher-income, white, well educated, middle-class, Republican, or conservative people expressed satisfaction with current spending levels. Marital status and gender had relatively little impact. Two variables—income and region—were particularly interesting because they had much greater effects on the elderly than on the younger age groups. Prosperous older people were conspicuously unsupportive of Social Security and Medicare increases, while elderly southerners were a good deal more supportive of increases than older people in other regions.

Attitudes toward government-funded medical insurance divided along similar lines in the 1984 NES data. Although the difference between age groups was almost negligible in the sample as a whole, substantial age differences did appear among certain subgroups. Older women, older Democrats and liberals, lower-income elderly people, and older people with less than a high school education were all much more favorable toward a government program of medical insurance than their younger peers. In contrast, older men and higher-income elderly people showed even less support for government medical insurance than their younger counterparts, while age differences disappeared among Republicans, conservatives and moderates, and high school graduates. Thus, disadvantaged and politically liberal groups of older people are conspicuous in their support for medical insurance, while the elderly in general are not.

The ABC News/*Washington Post* 1982 survey, because of its large sample of elderly persons, provided a good opportunity to examine the schisms among older people on aging policy issues—and schisms there were. Older respondents were sharply divided on the issue of general federal spending on the elderly, with those who favored increases opposing those who thought the government was spending enough already. Elderly Democrats, working-class people, blacks and Hispanics, and those with lower income and less education, were particularly likely to favor higher spending levels, in contrast to elderly Republicans, middle-class people, whites, the educated, and the wealthy. Older women, retirees, and liberals were also more favorable to government spending than were older men, conservatives, and the still-employed, although here the differences were smaller. Table 6 shows the differences among these subgroups of older people.

[5] See the appendix for coding of demographic and socioeconomic variables.

Table 6. Opinions Toward U.S. Government Spending on the Elderly, Persons 65 Years and Over, 1982 (Percent)

	Government Spends			
	Not Enough	Enough	Too Much	N
Income				
Low	53	38	8	448
High	30	57	13	151
Education				
<H.S. grad	56	35	10	210
H.S. grad	51	43	6	217
Some college	37	49	14	247
Social class				
Working	56	36	8	362
Middle	37	51	12	298
Sex				
Women	53	41	7	375
Men	41	45	14	305
Race				
White	46	44	10	579
Black/Hispanic	67	28	5	60
Retirement				
Retired	49	41	10	526
Employed	36	53	11	97
Marital status				
Married	44	44	12	365
Not married	51	41	8	315
Party				
Democrat	63	31	6	254
Independent	46	45	10	187
Republican	29	55	15	251
Ideology				
Liberal	56	38	6	173
Moderate	43	49	8	239
Conservative	44	41	15	243
Age				
65 to 74	50	42	8	487
75 and over	41	45	14	193

Source: ABC News/*Washington Post* Poll of Public Opinion on Aging, 1982. See appendix for exact question wording.

Gerontologists in recent years have distinguished between the "young-old"—the majority of people over sixty-five, who are healthy and active—and the "old-old"—those who are frail, mentally or physically impaired, and more in need of health and social services (see Neugarten and Hagestad 1976). The distinction is based more on social or physical traits than on chronological age, but many have suggested that seventy-five might be a more appropriate threshold age than sixty-five for aging policy purposes, since frailty and loss are much more common after the age of seventy-five. Objectively, people aged seventy-five and over might be more likely to support government benefits for the elderly, since they would be more likely to need such benefits than would the "young-old." However, Table 6 shows that respondents seventy-five years of age and over were less supportive of federal spending on the elderly than those between the ages of sixty-five and seventy-four.

None of these variables in the ABC News/*Washington Post* dataset had much effect on the issues of Medicare cutbacks and mandatory retirement. Since "increase spending" was not an option on the Medicare question, almost no one suggested that it should ever be cut back, although Democrats, liberals, and the less educated were a bit less willing to allow cutbacks due to the "financial crunch." As for mandatory retirement, majorities of all subgroups opposed it, although high school graduates, women, and the still working were somewhat more opposed than men, retirees, and the less educated.

How will the demographic and socioeconomic composition of the elderly affect the balance of opinion among the next few generations of older Americans? If the elderly remain divided along the same lines discussed here, the aggregate effects are likely to be mixed. The next few generations, as noted earlier, will be much better educated, a trait related to lower support for government spending on the elderly. At the same time, they will be more female, much older, and more likely to need continuous medical care for chronic health problems (Riche 1985). In addition, their household incomes, while continuing to grow, are not likely to keep pace with those of younger households (*American Demographics* 1984). These trends, along with the rising cost of medical care, could move older people to place increasing demands upon government.

Group Identification

Elderly group identification appears to have a positive effect on opinions toward old-age programs and benefits. Since 1972, the NES survey has asked respondents every four years whether they felt "particularly close to" a number of groups, including "older people."[6] Respondents then are asked which group they feel "closest to." For respondents sixty-five years and over, "older people" (or "the elderly") was the modal "closest" group in 1972, 1976, 1980, and 1984. The percentage who said they are closest to older people remained quite stable, varying between 30 and 37 percent. Thus, elderly group identification as measured by this question is relatively high among elderly people. Still, the percentage has failed to increase during the past decade, and the majority of older people feel closest to a variety of other groups—especially "middle-class people." NES respondents in 1984 were also asked, for the first time, which groups they felt close to, and closest to, "when it comes to economic matters." Again, the group most mentioned by people sixty-five and over was "the elderly"; 45 percent said they were the closest group.[7]

People in all age groups who felt psychologically or economically close to, or closest to, older people in 1984 were more likely to favor increased spending on Social Security and Medicare. In most cases the difference was one of 10 to 20 percent; this was true whether respondents felt closest to or merely close to older people. Interestingly, the effect was even more pronounced among the younger age groups, although of course fewer people in the younger categories chose older people as their closest group.

Group identification was also related to respondents' impressions of the most important national problem: seven percent of those who felt closest to the elderly in 1984 chose a problem related specifically to aging policy. Seven percent may not be a large number, but it is seven times greater than among those who felt closest to other groups. Thus, as found in previous studies, group identification is related to desire for more government attention to group-related problems. However, if elderly group identification itself is on the rise in the 1980s, along with their heightened media visibility and the growth of aging-based organizations, it is not evident in these data.

National, Group, and Personal
Economic Situation

How do people view the economic situation of their own family, their group, and their nation? How do these views affect their policy

---

[6] In 1984, "older people" was changed to "the elderly," making it perhaps less directly comparable to earlier years.

[7] This high percentage is rather suspect; respondents were not given a list of groups, but if at first they did not understand the question, they were given a few examples, among them "the elderly." Groups mentioned as examples might have been chosen by many respondents due to the power of suggestion (see Conover 1985).

positions, and which matters the most? The 1984 NES survey asked respondents to judge whether the nation, the elderly, and they themselves were economically better off, worse off, or about the same, compared to the previous year. In general, people were relatively upbeat about their own situations and that of the country; pluralities of over 40 percent said both were doing better. Only 10 percent were so optimistic about the elderly, however; a plurality thought the elderly were doing worse. Older people themselves were less pessimistic about the elderly as a group, but even they seemed to think the elderly were worse off than answers to the personal financial question would indicate.

All three types of assessments were related to people's opinions toward federal spending on Social Security and Medicare, according to an analysis of NES data. The worse the perceptions of national, elderly, or personal economic situations, the higher the approval rating of increases in these two programs. Like elderly group identification, economic assessments generally made a difference of 10 to 20 percentage points, across all three age groups. However, assessments of the national economy had the greatest effect and, surprisingly, perceptions of the elderly's group economic situation had the least effect of the three. Respondents' views of their own situation lay somewhere in between.

The ABC News/*Washington Post* survey did not ask about the economic situation of the elderly as a group, but it did ask respondents to predict whether they themselves, and the nation as a whole, would be economically better or worse off in the near future. Both types of assessments had a substantial effect on opinions toward government assistance for the elderly. Majorities of older respondents who felt that the national economy and their own finances would improve expressed satisfaction with current levels of funding; majorities of those who were pessimistic about the national economy and their own finances supported increased spending on the elderly. Here, respondents' assessments of their own situation had a slightly greater effect, as seen in Table 7.

Personal Situation

Perceptions of personal hardships do indeed affect older people's political attitudes. The ABC News/*Washington Post* survey asked additional questions permitting analysis of the relationship between older people's own situation and their opinions on aging policy. First, people were asked about their personal problems and how serious these problems were. Of these, "not having enough money to live on" and "not enough medical care" seemed particularly relevant to opin-

Table 7. Opinions Toward U.S. Government Spending on the Elderly, by National and Personal Economic Assessments, Persons 65 and Over, 1982 (Percent)

	Government Spends			
	Not Enough	Enough	Too Much	N
National economy				
Better	32	54	14	76
Same	36	52	12	142
Worse	54	38	8	444
Personal finances				
Better	27	58	14	77
Same	44	46	10	415
Worse	66	28	7	160

Source: ABC News/*Washington Post* Poll of Public Opinion on Aging, 1982. See appendix for exact question wording.

ions toward spending on the elderly and cutbacks in Medicare—and indeed they were. The seriousness of these personal problems for older people had a large effect on their opinions toward both issues, and especially toward spending on the elderly, as seen in Table 8. Most older people, however, did not report the lack of money and medical care as problems in their own lives.

Whether respondents themselves received government benefits for the aging, on the other hand, seemed to have little effect on their opinions toward government spending—except when the amount received was substantial. Opinions differed little between those who said they—or someone in their household—received Social Security, Medicare, or Medicaid, and those who did not. The same finding occurred for those with and without private pension income. However, attitudes toward federal spending on the elderly divided sharply between Social Security beneficiaries who received at least half their income from Social Security, and those whose income came primarily from other sources. Older beneficiaries who were dependent on Social Security for at least half their income ran three-to-two in favor of increased spending, while the rest ran three-to-two *against* spending increases, as also noted in Table 8.

Multivariate Analysis

We have seen that the diversity of older people reveals itself even in their attitudes toward aging policy issues. Older people often are di-

Table 8. Opinions Toward U.S. Government Spending on the Elderly, by
Personal Problems and Social Security Income, Persons 65 and Over, 1982
(Percent)

	Government Spends			
	Not Enough	Enough	Too Much	N
Money problems				
Very serious	88	12	0	43
Serious	79	18	3	71
Minor	57	36	7	130
No problem	35	52	13	434
Medical care				
Very serious	88	13	0	48
Serious	68	27	5	60
Minor	61	31	9	94
No problem	38	50	12	474
Social Security				
> Half of income	61	33	7	270
< Half of income	37	52	11	270

Source: ABC News/*Washington Post* Poll of Public Opinion on Aging, 1982. See appendix for exact question wording.

vided along social, demographic, ideological, and partisan lines on
these issues. Many of the variables related to older people's policy positions are, of course, also related to each other, and multivariate analysis can help isolate the variables that have a significant impact when
other independent variables are controlled. Again, the ABC News/
Washington Post 1982 survey, with its elderly oversample, provides a
reasonable number of cases for studying the divisions among older
people.

We will look at the effects of several variables on support for increasing government spending on the elderly.[8] Probit analysis is the
chosen statistical technique because, with a dichotomous or an ordinal
dependent variable, the probit model specifies a nonlinear form of relationship that need not meet the assumptions of the ordinary least
squares model (see Aldrich and Cnudde 1975; Aldrich and Nelson
1984; Hanushek and Jackson 1977, chapter 7; Wolfinger and Rosenstone 1980: 10–12; 121–23).

[8] The dependent variable has been dichotomized: the U.S. government is spending
"not as much as it should" on the elderly, versus "more than it should" or "as much as
it should."

Personal economic situation and political party identification are the most significant factors to emerge in this probit analysis. Table 9 lists the maximum likelihood estimate (MLE), standard error, and t-test statistic for each variable entered in the equation. Among the demographic and socioeconomic variables—income, education, social class, gender, age, race, retirement status, and marital status—only income is significant. Similarly, the subjective lack of "enough money to live on" and "enough medical care," as well as a pessimistic outlook toward personal finances in the following year, all have a significant effect on support for government spending on the elderly—but not amount of Social Security income or outlook on the national economy. Finally, party identification—but not ideology—has a significant impact on attitudes toward federal spending on the elderly.[9] Evidently, the lines that divide Americans on the issue of government benefits for the elderly are not generational, but economic and partisan.

Table 9. Probit Estimates of the Effect of Variables on Support for Increasing U.S. Government Spending on the Elderly, Persons 65 and Over, 1982

Variable	MLE	SE	t (MLE/SE)
Problem, medical care	.253	.087	2.92*
Problem, enough money	.212	.087	2.43*
Social Security > half income	−.044	.146	−0.30
National economy	.095	.102	0.93
Personal finances	.237	.115	2.05*
Political party I.D.	−.074	.033	−2.24*
Ideology	−.027	.064	−0.42
Education	.015	.054	0.29
Social class	−.143	.142	−1.01
Retirement status	.194	.152	1.27
Race	−.114	.233	−0.49
Income	−.128	.056	−2.29*
Sex	.107	.140	0.76
Marital status	−.236	.142	−1.67
Age	.005	.014	0.35
Constant	4.114	.544	7.57

Source: ABC News/*Washington Post* Poll of Public Opinion on Aging, 1982. See appendix for exact question wording and coding of variables.
Note: $N = 488$; *significant at .05 level.

[9] Several equations were run, using different codings on some variables, and/or dropping insignificant variables from the equation, for comparison purposes. In every case, the same five variables were significant at the .05 level.

Any interpretation of public opinion on political issues must be a cautious one; many studies have shown people's attitudes on political matters to be unstable, uninformed, and unreflective (e.g., Converse 1964). However, after examining data on a number of questions from different surveys, it appears that the divisions among older people in their opinions toward aging policy issues are many; their unity on group-related matters is, apparently, rather low.

CONCLUSION

Survey data on older Americans reveal little cohesion around, or commitment to, major aging-related issues. The deepest divisions among the elderly on these issues are economic and partisan. Older people who are poor, or who feel financially troubled, are more likely to support old-age government benefits than are prosperous, financially secure older people. Similarly, elderly Democrats are much more supportive of government aid than elderly Republicans. Political leaders wishing to mobilize the elderly around old-age issues must face these conflicts among older Americans.

Why, then, have leaders been so successful in building old-age political organizations? There are several possible reasons for current and even future organizational success. First, an explicit attitude-behavior link has never emerged from survey data analysis; there are too many intervening variables between political opinions and organizational activity. People join, and may even become active in organizations, for many reasons other than commitment to the organizations' stands on the issues, as we shall see in the next chapter. Second, even though organizational leadership may be more actively supportive of government intervention in aging policy issues than older people in general seem to be, this does not imply a large attitudinal gap or a lack of representation, as we shall see in chapter 6.

The apparent importance of personal problems, finances, and sources of income in their relation to attitudes toward aging policy is significant. The rising expectations of older people, in an era of vastly increased government expenditures on the elderly, could lead to frustration and resentment on their part as benefits are reduced and cost of living allowances cut back. Not only are older people painfully aware of their own problems, they are often likely to believe that most other older people face the same personal problems (O'Gorman 1980). Thus, as frustration grows, group consciousness is likely to grow, which is particularly significant at a time when partisan ties appear to be declining. Older people in the decades to come may continue to respond to mobilization efforts around old-age political issues.

Furthermore, there is little or no evidence that means-tested govern-ment benefits, restricted to people of demonstrated need rather than available to older people as a group, will ever be more popular among citizens of any age than universal old-age benefits. The aging-based organizations are likely to enjoy a large middle-class constituency, dedicated to the principles of social insurance, for many decades to come.

Perhaps the major dilemma for aging-based organizations today is the need to present a positive, optimistic image of older people as healthy, active, and affluent—a lucrative market for advertisers and a sector undeserving of age discrimination—at the same time that they work to convince policy makers that the elderly are a group in need of government assistance. But attracting members, despite diversity in at-titudes toward aging policy, is not likely to be a problem. The follow-ing chapters, on membership incentives, group political activity, and constituency representation, detail the reasons for predicting old-age organizational stability.

CHAPTER 4

Old-Age Interest Group Survival

POLITICAL organizations for the elderly have expanded tremendously, in both number and size, during recent decades. This is hardly surprising at first glance. Our society is aging rapidly; the over-sixty-five population is the fastest-growing age group, and will continue to be, well into the twenty-first century. Older people are healthier, wealthier, and better educated than ever. They enjoy a good deal of leisure time and energy for political activity, and their political interest is relatively high. Aging policy issues—especially Social Security and Medicare—frequently command the attention of politicians and the mass media. Older people have a large stake in government; they are the beneficiaries of 27 percent of the federal budget,[1] and they have much to defend.

Yet the long-term survival of the aging-based membership groups is not a foregone conclusion. Older people, as we saw in chapter 3, do not demonstrate much cohesion around, or commitment to, major aging-related issues. The elderly are highly diverse, and their political opinions register many divisions along demographic, socioeconomic, and partisan lines. People do not renounce their previous group affiliations upon turning sixty-five; ethnic, religious, occupational, social class, and other ties may be stronger, longer-lived, less stigmatized, and more politically prominent than those of old age. Diversity among the elderly is likely to grow as their numbers grow.

Furthermore, organizations like the major senior mass membership groups are facing a good deal of interest group competition in the 1980s. Recent studies of political organizations suggest that broad-based citizen groups with diverse memberships, after peaking during the 1970s, have since begun to decline in membership and resources (Salisbury 1983: 363–65). Their decline has coincided with the rise of three other types of political organizations: professional and service provider organizations, single-issue groups, and "staff" organizations with working staffs and financial patronage but no mass membership (Berry 1977; Cigler and Loomis 1983; Salisbury 1983; Walker 1983).

---

[1] Estimates for 1986 from the U.S. Office of Management and Budget. See U.S. Bureau of the Census (1987c: tables 480, 580).

Service provider organizations—including those of policy profession-als, social welfare agencies, and administrators at all levels of govern-ment—have proliferated along with government activities in aging and other policy areas. Staff organizations have profited from the increase in private foundations, philanthropists, and government grants. Sin-gle-issue groups have used mass media and communication technolo-gies to promote their causes and attract at least intermittent political action and donations from large numbers of citizens.

The expansion of one type of interest group, of course, need not lead to the demise of other types. Political organizations are not directly competitive in the sense that members must drop one group to join another; people can join as many organizations as they wish. The three types of groups now on the rise, however, could potentially cut into the advocacy and recruitment abilities of broad-based, multi-issue cit-izen groups. First, service provider and staff organizations may enjoy government connections not as open to broad-based membership groups. Many service provider groups include government employees and private sector individuals with professional acquaintances in gov-ernment. Staff organizations often run under the stewardship of gov-ernment grants or of well-connected wealthy individuals or founda-tions.

Second, many of the newer single-issue groups may cut into the po-tential membership pool with their targeted, urgent, and focused ap-peals, attracting some of the attention—and with it, the support—that might otherwise go to broad-based multi-issue groups. Among the old-age organizations discussed here, the National Committee to Preserve Social Security and Medicare—and, to some extent, the National Al-liance of Senior Citizens—are the two that could best be characterized as single-issue groups, because their issue focus is narrower than that of the other groups, and because they recruit members through the use of targeted direct mail.

Given these trends—the increasing diversity of older people and the apparent decline of broad-based multi-issue groups—can the current senior mass membership organizations survive? I will show in this chapter that such groups are likely to survive and flourish for decades to come. The argument covers three general aspects of group mainte-nance: (1) the recruitment and retention of organization members with the use of material, purposive, and solidary incentives; (2) the insider status of the organizations within the aging policy network; and (3) the degree of elite and general public support for old-age government programs and benefits supported by these organizations. The chapter also includes a discussion of the prospects and possible changes facing the major old-age membership organizations—in particular, the American Association of Retired Persons (AARP), the National Council of Senior Citizens (NCSC), the Gray Panthers, the National Committee to Preserve Social Security and Medicare (NCPSSM), and the National Alliance of Senior Citizens (NASC).

MEMBERSHIP INCENTIVES

The five major old-age organizations have memberships ranging from fifty thousand (Gray Panthers) to over twenty-eight million (AARP). Their memberships have expanded over the past several years, and many members participate in group political activities such as letter-writing campaigns, demonstrations, and committee work. What is the key to their success? More generally, how do political organizations attract, retain, and mobilize members on a mass scale?

Controversies abound over the origin and maintenance of mass membership political organizations, and a number of analysts have integrated these theoretical perspectives to generate "exchange theories" of interest groups. Organization leaders, or entrepreneurs, use a variety of incentives to promote membership and participation (e.g. Salisbury 1969; Wilson 1973; Moe 1980; Weissman 1970). Clark and Wilson's (1961) distinction between material, solidary, and purposive incentives has provided the most popular basis for studying organizational maintenance and growth in terms of exchange theory.

Political objectives lie at the heart of a political organization's origin and survival, since by definition such an organization works to influence public policy. It is usually difficult, however, to sustain a large membership on the basis of political objectives alone. When an organization achieves a political goal, many people beyond the organization's formal membership benefit from the result. If organizational pressure leads to higher Social Security benefits, for example, older people receive the higher benefits whether or not they are members of the organization. Thus, a group's potential members can benefit from the group's political successes without incurring the costs of joining the group; they become "free riders" (Olson 1965). To get around the free rider problem, mass membership political organizations offer their members other types of incentives to supplement the political reasons for joining and participating. AARP, NCSC, Gray Panthers, NCPSSM, and NASC all offer a variety of membership incentives, but they differ from one another in the types of benefits they emphasize.

Material Incentives

The tangible selective benefits offered to members serve as a major attraction to some of these organizations. AARP, one of the largest voluntary organizations of any type in the United States, offers the widest array of such benefits, and their appeal is clear. In a 1982 AARP membership survey cited by Paul Light (1985: 77) about the advantages of joining AARP, most mentioned the publications (including a newsletter and the magazine *Modern Maturity*); the discounts on insurance, drugs, and health aids; the travel club and the investment opportunities. Only 17 percent said they joined primarily because AARP "cared about and helped the elderly."

AARP is unusual among voluntary organizations in its heavy reliance on material benefits for members (Walker 1983: 396). In many ways, as one staff member for another organization noted, AARP is more like a "business" with "customers" than an organization with members. The organization advertises its consumer goods and services through various channels, including public television, newspapers and magazines, and direct mail. Some staffers with other organizations go so far as to charge AARP with using its nonprofit status to add to its commercial appeal.

But while AARP is the leader in material benefits, it does not have a monopoly among aging-based membership organizations. NCSC, the second largest and second oldest of these groups, also offers a monthly newsletter, drug and insurance discounts, and planned vacation tours. NASC features many of the same types of publications, discounts, and services, including a heavily advertised insurance plan, and NCPSSM, the newest of the organizations, also has begun to offer volume discounts and group insurance. Only the Gray Panthers, whose leaders emphasize political commitment over size, are not offered material incentives beyond their monthly newsletter.

Solidary Incentives

Some people may join political organizations, in part, for the opportunity to meet and socialize with other people with similar interests, and to gain personal prestige and praise for their activities and leadership roles. The Gray Panthers and NCSC emphasize these aspects of group membership much more than the other groups. The Gray Panthers started out as a loose alliance of local chapters, or "networks," and the group continues to stress the importance of local autonomy and voluntary activity despite a more recent movement toward national centralization and coordination. NCSC also began as a federation of local senior citizen clubs and retired member organizations; the local affiliates now number about 4,500. While NCSC now recruits some members through direct mail techniques, it still attempts as much as possible to recruit through local clubs and to direct new national members to the local affiliates. Meeting with fellow members, group leaders believe, enhances interest in group political participation.

At the other extreme, the two newer groups, NASC and NCPSSM, began recruiting from their national offices by direct mail and mass communication, and have established few state and local chapters where members can meet together. AARP, with fewer than ten percent of its members belonging to its 3,700 local chapters, has been diverting more resources and energy in recent years toward the development of local affiliates, regular chapter meetings, and local committee work.

Purposive Incentives

Purposive incentives provide the satisfaction of supporting a cause, and as such they are more conducive to political activity and commitment within the organization. At the same time, purposive incentives are more sporadic and unstable as sources of member recruitment and retention. A group that depends on expressive benefits for its members is most vulnerable to disagreements over political issues, and to members' loss of interest as political conditions change (Moe 1980; Cigler and Hansen 1983: 102). The satisfaction that comes from supporting a cause has a highly elastic utility, and is unlikely to promote steady contributions over a long period of time (Hardin 1982).

One advantage of material and solidary incentives is that, once members join for those reasons, their continuing membership and participation may become more politically motivated—that is, more responsive to purposive incentives. Members who join in order to receive material benefits, for example, become more aware of the issues by reading the group's publications; awareness often breeds concern. Awareness also increases through meeting with fellow members, and social pressure within the group often encourages collective activity. Members who join for nonpolitical reasons may remain for largely political ones (Franke and Dobson 1985: 229; Salisbury 1975: 199).

Groups that emphasize purposive incentives over the other types tend to be smaller in size. Punnett (1971) distinguished between "sectional" groups, which base their strength and authority on the large proportion of constituents they represent, and "cause" groups, which stress members' political commitment over membership size. AARP is a prime example of a sectional group; many of its members may not be actively involved in aging political issues, but the backing of twenty-eight million members means a lot to many local, state, and national politicians. When AARP initiates a letter drive to members of Congress, even a fraction of its membership can flood the Capitol mailboxes. The Gray Panthers, in contrast, represents itself as a cause group, and recruits members on this basis. Gray Panther activists have repeated the sentiments of Panther leader Maggie Kuhn, who wrote (1976: 91):

> [W]e recognize that we cannot hope to motivate everybody over 65 to join our movement. We have modest goals and hopes for the enlistment of small numbers of wrinkled radicals who are fully committed people, willing to engage in controversy and take the risks involved.

Observers of interest group activity disagree over which of these approaches is more conducive to organizational maintenance and stability. Moe (1980), for example, suggests that an emphasis on political causes can be destabilizing, making a group prone to policy disputes, division into splinter groups, and the loss of members who lose interest in the leaders' political priorities. Pratt, on the other hand, argues that "purposive incentives . . . have been a primary source of senior-citizen cohesiveness" (1976: 199). Member apathy toward aging policy issues in recent years could lead to a decline in organizational influence and appeal, despite the groups' size, wealth, legitimacy, committed leadership, and low degree of factionalism (Pratt 1983: 168–78). Both analyses are probably correct. A high degree of political interest and activity among organization members *can* be destabilizing when there are policy disputes, but can also enhance member gratification and group visibility if disputes can be avoided.

One thing lacking in the political attraction of these organizations is a single, dramatic issue to rally around. The rise of single-issue interest groups indicates the importance of the unifying issue for mass appeal. The two newer organizations, NASC and NCPSSM, are the most similar to single-issue groups; both have used mass mailings to draw attention to a particular dramatic cause: the imminent "crisis" of Social Security and Medicare. NASC, conservative in orientation, calls itself "the national organization for responsible seniors," and urges cutbacks in most federal aid programs, including those for the elderly. NCPSSM has appealed for donations and for letters and petitions to Congress, with messages that most other group leaders and policy makers have characterized as slick, hard-sell "scare tactics" (see also Fessler 1984). Both NASC and NCPSSM have been successful in attracting hundreds of thousands of responses and donations, and certainly they are not the only groups to send out urgent messages in mass mailings. Yet few policy elites are aware of NASC's existence, and many have denounced NCPSSM's tactics as largely negative, misleading, and insincere. It seems that the dramatic single-issue approach, while successful at first, may be fleeting in its appeal and low in political prestige.

The other three organizations—AARP, NCSC, and the Gray Panthers—have differed from each other, and over time, in the issues they publicize most forcefully. Both AARP and the Gray Panthers, for example, have been strong advocates of uncapping mandatory retirement, while NCSC, with its largely retired union and blue-collar membership, has been more ambivalent on the issue. NCSC has pressed for the maintenance and growth of federal aid to all older people; AARP has been more supportive of voluntary action and private sector involvement; the Gray Panthers organization has emphasized the targeting of poor and minority subgroups of older people in federal aid programs (Pratt 1983).

The major broad issues have changed for all three groups over the years. In the 1970s, income maintenance and preservation of Social Security cost-of-living allowances dominated; in the 1980s it was health care cost and quality. Yet two themes have constantly stood out—and they are, many policy makers insist, contradictory demands. All three groups oppose age discrimination and age-segregating programs, yet all advocate special benefits and services for older people. Policy makers may grumble, but organization leaders are wise to espouse both of these broad goals while negotiating in reality over policy details. Older people are attracted to both the civil rights policy of less discrimination, and the social welfare policy of more benefits.

One other trend has, to a large degree, united these three groups and rallied their members around political issues: the shift from expansion to defense of benefits for older people. Over the past two decades, federal benefits for the elderly—most notably, Social Security—have expanded; poverty among older people has declined; and the elderly have become one of the government's major claimant groups. Now that they have such a large stake in government, and are accustomed to the benefits they receive, older people are more responsive than ever to purposive incentives. Hardin (1982: 62–64) has listed several reasons why collective action to oppose a loss is easier to motivate than cooperation to support a gain. The goal is more clearly focused, the moral reaction to potential inequity is stronger, the perception of fairness outweighs that of selfishness, and losses are felt more acutely than gains of comparable magnitude. As long as old-age benefits are threatened by federal deficits, slow economic growth, and increasing numbers of older people—all of which seem probable for decades to come—purposive incentives are likely to be more appealing than during earlier eras of expansion.

Recruitment

Publicizing incentives and recruiting members is easier than ever for organizations today, with the use of computerized mailing lists and mass media. There is the danger, with these recruitment techniques, that organizations purporting to represent a large number of people are actually staff organizations with isolated, uninformed, and uncommitted "members" who have simply written a check and signed a form letter (Hayes 1983, 1986). This is probably more true, however, of the newer groups than of the older, more established groups that are using mass mailing techniques to supplement, not supplant, local and face-to-face recruitment efforts.

Older people, in general, are likely to become more active and open to political appeals over the next several decades. Older people are increasingly numerous, healthy, and better educated. Their declining attachments to political parties could lead to increased interest group involvement as a substitute (Cutler 1981). Despite their better health and longer life, the decades-old trend toward earlier retirement is not likely to reverse itself (Kosterlitz 1986a), so more older people will have leisure time and will be seeking activities to replace their work roles. Older people do not disengage from political activity; they are, compared to other age groups, active in organizations; they are joiners (Hudson and Strate 1985: 555; Babchuck et al. 1979; S. Cutler 1977). Furthermore, the organizations do not confine themselves to members over sixty-five years of age. Capitalizing on general public support for Social Security, Medicare, and elderly benefits in general, most groups do not have age limits, and AARP has lowered its age eligibility to fifty years.

But what about the diversity of older people? If they are likely to be politically active for decades to come, it does not follow that they will necessarily be active in aging-based organizations. However, as we have seen, the organizations themselves are diverse. They may all claim to represent older people as a whole, but they are different, and so are their memberships. The competition among the groups is less fierce than it was a decade ago. There is more agreement among them about issues—at least among AARP, NCSC, and the Gray Panthers—largely due to their defensive stance now, and they respect each other's positions in the aging policy network (Pratt 1982: 32). They all claim to be concentrating on broadening their memberships to include more minorities and more women in leadership roles. Furthermore, to the extent that the groups do disagree, their "lack of a unified front may also be a source of strength," as each group advocates for its particular priorities among the variety of elderly programs (Peirce and Choharis 1982: 1562; see also Freeman 1975: 51). A few years ago, Pratt (1982: 32) wrote that "only the views of the far right appear to be missing from the basic political stance of any of the old-age organizations." Now that NASC has emerged with a mass membership, the right wing is covered as well. There seems to be something for everyone.

MASS MEMBERSHIP ORGANIZATIONS IN THE AGING POLICY NETWORK

A large membership sustained over several years is one measure of success for mass-based political organizations, but not the only one. Their ability to attract the attention and sympathy of policy elites is also important to their image, and important to the credibility of purposive incentives.

Organizations on the road to stability and political influence generally pass through a series of steps, first building up and consolidating their internal structure, membership, and resources, and then devoting more of these resources to external relations and political goals (Williamson et al. 1982: 93–96; Pratt 1982). The old-age mass membership organizations are in varying stages of development in the mid-1980s, ranging from early stages of foundation-building and consolidation, to a more advanced, institutional stage featuring sophisticated, coordinated, and pragmatic politics. The older, institutionalized organizations—primarily AARP and NCSC—are now well entrenched in the federal aging policy network, while NCPSSM and NASC are still trying to achieve stable memberships and respect within the policy community. The Gray Panthers group is somewhere in between, having gained the respect of policy makers without achieving the Washington insider status of AARP and NCSC.

Intergroup differences in status and legitimacy are not functions of the age of the groups alone. These five organizations have not followed the same path of development, and it is not yet clear whether they will end up at a similar institutionalized phase after a certain number of years in operation. AARP got its start as primarily a service group, becoming more politically active after it was an established membership organization. NCSC and the Gray Panthers built their political organizations largely at the grass roots and local level, though coordinated out of the national offices.

NCPSSM and NASC, on the other hand, started out as computerized direct mail operations. Each has signed up more than a million members—over five million in the case of NCPSSM—and each has raised millions of dollars from membership dues and contributions alone. In addition, NCPSSM has flooded congressional offices with postcards, form letters, and petitions signed by people on their mailing lists, urging members of Congress to "save" Social Security and Medicare. The mailings have been massive, yet for some reason mail from the NCPSSM does not seem to carry the same credibility as, for example, AARP's letter-writing campaigns. Mass mailings from AARP and NCSC are perceived as signs of constituency interest and concern; they are taken quite seriously. Letters from NCPSSM have been described by congressional staff persons as "irritating, not effective." "They bludgeon members [of Congress] to death with postcards," said another staffer; "they lack sincerity"; "they claim credit [for policy influence] after the fact"; "they scare their members into writing to us," others said. NASC is much less well known, but staffers who had heard of NASC expressed the same sentiments about lack of sincerity and legitimacy.

What lies behind such reactions? What do AARP, NCSC, and the Gray Panthers have that the other two do not? Two things, apparently, make the difference in policy makers' perceptions: an active, informed presence on Capitol Hill and an informed, stable mass membership.

AARP and NCSC are institutionalized organizations in the Weberian sense: they are centralized and hierarchical, with differentiated structures and professional staffs of policy experts. They have secularized leadership without divisive leadership battles, and they have gained support from government grants and private foundations (Pratt 1976; Hudson and Strate 1985: 572). The Gray Panthers group is more decentralized and informally structured but now realizes the value of formal structure and national coordination and has taken steps in this direction (Jacobs 1980). It has also gained a great deal of mass media attention and has the reputation of attracting a relatively small but committed and sincere membership.

Federal agency officials and congressional staff members listed several reasons for the rise in prominence of these groups. Many noted that the groups—AARP and NCSC in particular—have become more sophisticated and pragmatic in their politics, engaging "top-notch" lobbyists and offering expert testimony and position papers. Many of their lobbyists and staff members, in fact, have come to the organizations from congressional aging committee staffs and federal agencies. The groups have moved from the position of outside agitators to that of legitimate insiders; they have "carved their own niche" in the aging policy circles in Washington. They have become an "effective countervailing force" to such powerful lobbies as the American Medical Association and the Federation of American Hospitals.

Republicans and Democrats alike expressed appreciation for the information and help they have received from organization representatives. "They offer viable solutions," one congressional staffer said; "they don't just whine about the problems"; and they are willing to compromise and negotiate. Some interviewees also pointed out that a few of the aging-based groups have become more adept at fundraising and have recently begun to form political action committees. Many were impressed by the stature and prestige of organization spokespersons. The leadership of Save Our Security—a coalition of senior, liberal, and labor organizations opposed to reductions in Social Security benefits—has included Washington luminaries Arthur Flemming, Wilbur Cohen, and Robert Ball. Gray Panthers founder Maggie Kuhn commands much respect, if not always agreement on political views, as did the late founders of the Older Women's League, Tish Sommers and Laurie Shields. Furthermore, if the Gray Panthers are perceived as more radical and less willing to compromise than AARP and NCSC, many policy makers recognize them as active suitors of public opinion through grass roots work and media events. "The mainstream organizations are glad the Panthers are there," one congressional staff member said. "They say what the others can't say," keeping radical proposals visible while "the others" work out concessions and compromises.

Also impressive to policy makers are the huge memberships of the aging groups; again, AARP and NCSC stand out. Not only do they have the numbers, they also have the ability to mobilize massive letter-writing and telephone campaigns at short notice when key legislation is in committee or on the floor. Some congressional staff members said that local chapters of the national organizations are able to draw large turnouts at meetings and forums and to publicize aging issues widely at election time, pressuring individual members of Congress. The national organizations can also mobilize large rallies and demonstrations in Washington, attracting media attention. As one official pointed out, the aging groups can sustain interest in successive issues and long-term goals; they do not die out with single-issue campaigns. Some policy makers recognize that the groups' stands on federal benefits for the elderly are often more liberal than those of most older Americans. Many, however, perceive the organizations as largely representative of their members' views—as long as there is evidence of constituency support at the state or district level, supplemented by expert lobbying at the national level. Policy makers are, by and large, suspicious of direct mail operations conducted from a small national office.

The national prominence of AARP, NCSC, and the Gray Panthers in aging policy circles is much less evident at the state government level. The involvement of state and local governments in aging policy issues, however, is growing. Although the major entitlement programs—Social Security and Medicare—are federally funded and administered, the state and local governments have gradually taken on more responsibility for the administration of many programs affecting the elderly, such as Medicaid, long-term care, and social services provided under the Older Americans Act.

Broad-based organizations with nationally dispersed constituencies such as those of the aging have, in general, lobbied more effectively at the national level. At the lower levels of government they tend to face more intense intergroup competition over more limited resources. Narrower, locally concentrated commercial and professional interests are more likely to dominate (Estes 1979: 209; McFarland 1983; Peirce and Choharis 1982: 1561). This view was supported by interviews with administrators and legislative staff in Sacramento, California, where almost no one judged the senior organizations as effective or influential actors in state aging politics. One state official called AARP "a joke" in state politics; another said the senior organizations offered "no constructive ideas." State policy makers were more impressed with the political savvy of service providers and professional groups in the aging field. Some did acknowledge that the aging organizations were beginning to increase their visibility, but only recently.

California is of course not representative of all fifty states. Throughout the twentieth century, however, aging organizational activity has probably been more intense in California than in any other state (Fischer 1979: 57; Lammers 1983: 59). Thus the relative weakness of mass membership aging organizations in Sacramento is probably typical of other state capitals. Some congressional districts in the United States have large communities of retirees—southern Florida is a prime example—where older people exert a good deal of influence in local and state politics (Peirce and Choharis 1982: 1559). However, even in Florida, with the highest proportion of seniors, old-age activism at the local level is isolated, sporadic, and "does not appear to have a major impact on most cities and counties" (Rosenbaum and Button 1987: 15). Group leaders and staff members of all five organizations expressed awareness of this weakness, and all claimed that they were beginning to allocate much more energy and more resources toward building up their state and local organizational networks. AARP, NCSC, and the Gray Panthers already have networks in place in most states.

Given more time, will NCPSSM and NASC develop the local networks and institutional connections enjoyed by the other three organizations? NCPSSM probably has a better chance than NASC, which was founded in 1974 but is still hardly recognized on Capitol Hill. NCPSSM, founded in 1982, has increased its staff to about thirty—including at least one hired away from AARP—and is stepping up its lobbying efforts in addition to the direct mail solicitations. Some policy makers recognize and appreciate the change; indeed, there was some perceptible positive change in opinion toward NCPSSM between the 1985 interviews and those of 1986.

PUBLIC SUPPORT FOR OLD-AGE BENEFITS

The elderly, because of the many large interest groups that lobby in their behalf, and because of the many government benefits and programs that are age-based, are often characterized as a "special interest." Yet there is not much evidence of intergenerational conflict; most aging benefits enjoy tremendous support from the public as a whole. The elderly are a highly legitimate welfare group; as one congressional staffer put it, old-age benefits are "still apple pie and motherhood." There are three major reasons for such extensive support. First, almost everyone is ultimately affected by old-age policy. Younger adults are concerned not only about their own future as retirees, but they are also concerned about their own parents and other elderly family members, who would often rely on more economic support from the family were it not for government support (Myles 1984: 170). Second, the belief that many older people are poor and needy remains widespread (Light 1985: 59), despite the fact that proportionately fewer people sixty-five and over today live below the poverty line compared to the population as a whole. This belief is not totally off the mark, since a larger proportion of older people lives *near* poverty.

Third, there is in this country a great deal of support for the social insurance principle, as opposed to public assistance. Social Security and Medicare—by far the largest and most widely supported programs for older people—are based on contributions paid into the system during a person's working life. Workers "earn" their rights to old-age benefits; thus they do not carry the stigma of means-tested public assistance (Brown 1984: 121; Light 1985: 60). According to several people involved in national aging policy, the major aging-based interest groups have capitalized on this sentiment during the past decade or two in two ways. First, they have increasingly emphasized the image of older people as deserving rather than needy, as assets and contributors to society. Second, they have broadened their membership appeal to preretirement or even younger adults. Some interviewees felt that the direct-mail organizations, NASC and NCPSSM, also capitalized on the popularity of old-age benefits by jumping on the elderly bandwagon. Their mass mailings, some suspect, are conducted primarily to raise funds for their organizations, and not out of sincere concern for the older people; thus the doubts about those groups' legitimacy.

Financial and logistic support from private foundations and government agencies has also expanded the resources of AARP, NCSC, and the Gray Panthers. Researchers have found that such support is crucial to many, if not most, voluntary organizations today (Walker 1983; Zald and McCarthy 1979). As federal involvement has increased in the aging field, elderly organizations have become valuable allies to federal employees whose careers are tied to political support for their programs. Thus these organizations have gained preferential access to government policy makers and administrators, as well as some government funding for their role as middlemen in helping to administer social services.

If public support is so high for old-age benefits, why do older people even need political organizations? There is, among certain groups and policy elites, evidence of political backlash against government benefits based solely on old age. Some analysts and policy makers involved in aging policy issues are grumbling about the large share of the federal budget going to the elderly—many of them quite well off—at a time when the budget needs to be trimmed. A small but vocal group called Americans for Generational Equity has been promoting such solutions as taxing Social Security benefits and encouraging private retirement plans. Some minority leaders have expressed concern about old-age benefits going primarily to white middle-class older people, leaving less for younger groups which are more heavily black and Hispanic (Torres-Gil 1986). Opposition to aging-based benefits can come from both the Right—concerned about "big government" and federal deficits—and the Left—favoring more benefits for the poor and minorities.

Such opposition may actually do more to promote the survival and maintenance of aging-based mass membership groups than to obstruct them. People are more responsive to threatened losses than to calls for new and expanded benefits (Carlie 1969; Freeman 1975; Hansen 1985). In fact, the senior political movement suffered a long sluggish period in the 1940s and 1950s, after Social Security was passed and the earlier aging-based organizations lost their momentum and raison d'être (Fischer 1979; Wilson 1973: 207). Some organization leaders today say that they welcome the opposition as a shot in the arm for member participation.

ADAPTING TO THE FUTURE

Despite their differences, the old-age mass membership organizations share a number of advantages that help secure their maintenance and survival. Their political appeal to their members and to the general public is based on both "special" interest and "public" interest. The array of membership incentives offered by these groups is especially important to old-age organizational maintenance, and these organizations—particularly AARP—are famous for their allure. The elderly, as a beneficiary group, enjoy a high degree of public support, and there is enough of a threat to enhance their organizations' sense of purpose. Three of them—AARP, NCSC, and the Gray Panthers—are well entrenched in the aging policy community and command a good deal of respect and legitimacy from policy elites. All of these factors—membership incentives, public support, and connections with policy makers—enhance organizational stability in the face of a divided and often apathetic constituency.

What will happen in future years if some of these organizational advantages are removed? All three types of incentives could be vulnerable to future trends; all three types may be available to members from other sources. Material incentives such as the publications, insurance, health aids, travel clubs, and investment plans may become more widely available on the private market, as companies compete for business from the growing numbers of older people with leisure time and disposable income (Lazer 1985). Solidary incentives may become less important as the older population grows in numbers, diversity, and outside activity, and as more opportunities present themselves for other types of political and nonpolitical group activities. Finally, the appeal of purposive incentives may decrease as older people—especially the middle- and upper-middle-class elderly who are more likely to join organizations in the first place—find a greater number of alternatives to government benefits, including IRAs, more widely available and adequate private pensions, assets including home ownership, and more widely available private medical insurance and health maintenance organizations. With alternatives available elsewhere, members are more likely to leave than to stay and try to change their organizations; they are, in Albert O. Hirschman's words, more likely to use "exit" than "voice" (Hirschman 1970).

Private market or no, however, AARP's selective benefits are likely to attract and retain members for a long time. AARP is like an established business, with many private sector connections, and with such a wide array of benefits for the five dollar annual dues, that market competition is unlikely to put it out of business. Its political activities, and the political concerns of its members, will ebb and flow with the importance of aging policy issues, but its business activities will sustain the large membership and staff of lobbyists and political experts.

NCSC's major assurance of survival is probably its institutional basis in the labor movement. NCSC was established by organized labor, and although its membership has expanded beyond retired union members, it still receives most of its support and its leadership from the unions. In fact, NCSC is not just dependent on organized labor any more; it is one of the elements that keeps the labor movement viable. The proportion of American workers belonging to labor unions has declined over the past several years, while the number of retired union members continues to expand. The Miners Union, for example, now has more retired members than members who are still working, according to one group leader. The retirees, furthermore, are more politically active than retired union members have ever been in the past.

The Gray Panthers group is the most likely of all the aging-based organizations to suffer the problems of social movements: divisiveness over political priorities, splintering into subgroups, loss of interest as issues are partially resolved or superseded by other issues, and the problem of eventually replacing a charismatic leader—Maggie Kuhn—who has come to be strongly identified with the movement. The Panthers, however, are also most likely to profit from the emerging backlash against old-age benefits, since their primary rhetorical cause has always been intergenerational equity and cooperation, and the targeting of groups based on need rather than on age. The Panthers may actually head off conservative groups like Americans for Generational Equity, preventing the right wing from monopolizing the view that affluent older people should not be so heavily subsidized by the government.

The future of NCPSSM and NASC will provide an interesting lesson not only for the aging movement but, even more, for the multitude of direct-mail political operations that have emerged with new communications technologies during the past few years. Their experience thus far indicates that such groups eventually need to supplement their mailing lists and media blitzes with policy experts, lobbyists, and some form of membership meetings, if they are to gain stability and legitimacy in the eyes of policy makers. Direct-mail political tactics may acquire a legitimacy of their own in future years as they become more widespread and established; however, it does not seem likely in the near future.

Specialized organizations for the aging that are narrower in scope are numerous and likely to remain in service for a long time. These include professional organizations such as the National Council on the Aging and the Gerontological Society of America; occupational groups such as the National Association of Retired Federal Employees; groups based on race or ethnicity such as the National Caucus and Center on Black Aged and the Asociación Nacional pro Personas Mayores; women's groups such as the Older Women's League; and private foundations lobbying in behalf of the elderly poor such as the Villers Foundation. Some of these groups are mostly professional; a few, most notably the Older Women's League and the National Association of Retired Federal Employees, have a large national membership. All of the organizations mentioned are well regarded on Capitol Hill and in the federal agencies, and their existence makes sense in light of the diversity of the older population. However, they are not likely ever to supplant the mass membership organizations, because they lack the array of membership incentives and the mass mobilizational ability that the large membership groups have developed.

But if the survival and maintenance of the mass membership senior organizations seems assured, what about their influence and their representativeness? Are these organizations too liberal to represent accurately the views of older Americans, given that survey data show older people to be less supportive of old-age benefit increases than younger adults? On the other hand, will the groups' current defensive stance stifle aging policy innovation and redistribution to the most needy? To answer these questions requires an examination of both sides of the groups' intermediary role in old-age politics. One side is the organizations' influence upon aging policy; the other side is the organizations' representation of constituency needs. These issues are discussed in the following chapters.

CHAPTER 5

Interest Groups and Aging Policy

How powerful is the gray lobby? Old-age interest groups appear to be one of the great political success stories of the last two decades. The number of groups has proliferated, their memberships continue to grow, and their lobbying techniques have gained in sophistication and legitimacy in the eyes of policy makers. Federal spending on programs and benefits for older Americans increased from under 15 percent of the federal budget, to an estimated 27 percent, between 1960 and 1986. The poverty rate among the elderly was halved from 28.5 percent in 1966 to 14.6 percent in 1982 (U.S. Senate, Special Committee on Aging, 1984: 2), and has continued to drop.

The elderly have made impressive policy gains; many government programs either are explicitly age-based or disproportionately benefit the elderly. During the past two and a half decades, for example, Congress passed Medicare, Medicaid, and the Older Americans Act; it expanded housing assistance to the elderly and abolished mandatory retirement; Social Security benefits were increased and tied to the cost of living; Supplemental Security Income established a minimum income for the elderly; and committees advising on aging policy matters were institutionalized in Congress and the executive branch.

The growth of the aging policy system is evident in Congress, in the executive branch, and at state and local levels of government. Even in the 1980s—a period of retrenchment, budget deficits, and cutbacks in domestic spending—politicians were reluctant to tamper with programs and entitlements for the elderly. Among federal programs funded by discretionary domestic spending, social services for the aging have suffered the least from budget cuts (U.S. Senate, Special Committee on Aging 1984: 14). All this conjures up images of a powerful lobby backed by a broad constituency of older Americans.

The image of a powerful senior lobby, however, is open to dispute. Despite the political achievements of senior advocates, many millions of older people remain economically insecure. The elderly are more likely than any other adult age group to live in poverty; they are more likely than the population as a whole to live below 125 percent of the poverty level (U.S. Bureau of the Census 1987b, 1988). The political benefits that the elderly have enjoyed, furthermore, are not necessarily the work of aging-based organizations. Other political influences, such as government officials, allied organizations, or sympathetic public opinion, may deserve as much or more of the credit for aging policy achievements than the elderly's own interest groups.

There is in fact much debate in the literature over the role and influence of interest groups, in aging policy as well as in other policy areas. The purpose of this chapter is to examine the relative influence of the aging-based organizations upon aging policy since the 1960s, when present-day organizations became politically active. The influence of the elderly interest groups has increased greatly relative to other interest groups—both opponents and allies. There are, however, limitations to this influence when viewed in the larger context of political forces within the American system.

The chapter begins with a look at changes in the economic and social well-being of the elderly during the last few decades, in order to assess the impact of aging policy on the lives of older Americans. Overall, their situation has improved markedly, but their economic diversity has increased as well, with many remaining in poverty or near-poverty. The second part of the chapter traces the evolution of interest group power within the aging policy network, from the 1960s to the present. There is sometimes a distinction, as we will see, between those who influence policy and those who benefit; knowing the latter does not lead automatically to the identification of the former. The chapter ends with a discussion of future prospects for the aging-based interest groups, particularly as the "baby boom" generation ages and swells the ranks of the retired by the middle of the twenty-first century.

OLD AGE IN THE 1980S: ECONOMIC AND SOCIAL WELL-BEING

Public policy and private pensions have improved the economic situation of older Americans during the second half of the twentieth century. Changes have been so dramatic in recent decades, that the stereotype of the impoverished aged, ravaged by inflation, is being replaced by a new stereotype: that of affluent retirees imposing a burden on the national economy (Binstock 1983). Still, whether measured in terms of finance, health, retirement, or subjective well-being, the hardships and opportunities of old age in America remain complex and controversial. As in any area of public policy, partisans of every viewpoint can manipulate the numbers to prove their point. The diversity of older people makes generalizations difficult, and therefore suspect.

The poverty rate has declined considerably for those sixty-five and over; more than a third lived in poverty in 1959, compared to about one in eight in 1987 (U.S. Bureau of the Census 1987b, 1988). The poverty rate for the elderly fell below that of the population as a whole for the first time in 1982. Inflation, furthermore, is no longer the problem it used to be for older people living on fixed incomes. Since the bulk of income going to most elderly households—including Social Security benefits, federal Supplemental Security Income, food stamps, and civil service and military pensions—contains automatic cost-of-living adjustments, older people tend to be less vulnerable to inflation than the rest of the population. Financial assets and private pensions, important sources of income for older people—including many who are near but not below the poverty line—do remain vulnerable to inflation, however (Schulz 1988: 56–61, 256).

These poverty estimates are based on money income only. Poverty rates for older people decline even further, and the median income gap between aged and nonaged adults narrows, when noncash government benefits and special tax provisions are factored into the calculations. The effects are controversial, however; there is no officially accepted method for including such benefits in poverty and income statistics. Including food, energy, and housing benefits, for example, reduces the elderly poverty rate by one or two percentage points. Adding medical benefits reduces the elderly poverty rate by another seven percentage points, to about 3 percent (U.S. Bureau of the Census 1987a).

The problem with adding in-kind benefits to the calculation of poverty rates is that no generally accepted value exists for these benefits. Recipients themselves, for example, may value these benefits less than what would be indicated by market prices (Schulz 1988: 2, 42). Estimates that include noncash benefits are open to charges of bias, such as the Villers Foundation accusation (1987: 20) that researchers using this method "end up arguing for an untenable proposition: that the more costly health care is for a particular group, the lower the poverty rate."

Not only is the methodology questionable; the officially defined poverty index, based on very minimal standards, is itself controversial (Schulz 1988: 45–50). Persons who are "near-poor"—up to 200 percent of the poverty level—are arguably struggling to get by. People sixty-five years and over are more likely than the population as a whole to live below 125 percent of the poverty level, and are 25 percent more likely to live below 200 percent of poverty (U.S. Bureau of the Census 1987b; Villers Foundation 1987: 18–23).

Such data on poverty levels, complex as they may be, still do not capture the objective financial well-being of older people. Indeed, when viewed in terms of asset ownership, older people appear relatively affluent. The median net worth of households headed by persons sixty-five and over was $60,266 in 1984, compared to $32,667 for all households (U.S. Bureau of the Census 1986). Similarly, median income figures can be used to "prove" that older people are poorer than the nonelderly—when calculated on a household basis—or richer than the nonelderly—when calculated on a per capita basis—because elderly households tend to be smaller (Villers Foundation 1987: 28–29).

All of these measures of central tendency ignore the most important factor in discussing older people's economic well-being: the wide divergence in income among the aged. They vary at least as widely as younger Americans; some analysts estimate that there is more inequality among the elderly than among the nonelderly (Smeeding 1986). The diversity is such that many government policies benefit some older people while adversely affecting others. Low-income older people, for example, suffered the most from early Reagan administration policies that emphasized program and benefit reductions (Storey 1983). A few years later, changes in Social Security and Medicare saddled the affluent elderly with benefit taxes and surcharges based on personal income. Funds saved through Social Security benefits taxation and other 1983 changes, as well as through Medicare cuts, have helped to finance recent increases in Supplemental Security Income and Medicaid—both programs targeting the poor (Haas 1987: 2415). Thus different groups have benefited at different times, but the end result is that inequality among older people remains high relative to other age groups.

An international perspective on aging in six industrial nations illustrates even more vividly the degree of inequality among older Americans.[1] Looking at disposable family income adjusted for household size, Smeeding and Torrey (1987) conclude that older people in the United States enjoy higher incomes relative to the national average than in any other country studied. At the same time, the income inequality among the U.S. elderly is greater than in any of the other five countries, resulting in an old-age poverty rate that is second highest among the six countries.

Harsh economic conditions are particularly concentrated among certain groups of older people: women, minorities, persons living alone, and the oldest old—those over eighty-five years of age. Older blacks in 1985 were nearly three times as likely, and older Hispanics

[1] Canada, West Germany, Norway, Sweden, the United Kingdom, and the United States.

twice as likely, to be poor as were elderly whites. Older women suffered twice the poverty rate of older men, and three times that rate if they lived alone. Finally, poverty among persons eighty-five years and over was 50 percent higher than among those sixty-five years and over. People with two or more of these characteristics suffer the severest of conditions; for example, the majority (54 percent) of older black women living alone were poor in 1985 (Villers Foundation 1987: 15–16). These figures reflect inequalities throughout the life cycle that are perpetuated and often magnified in old age.

Despite the economic diversity, there is no question that the aged as a group have seen their standard of living increase, and their poverty rate decline, more than other age groups in recent years. The poverty rate of children, in particular, has risen the most of any age group, as the elderly poverty rate has declined. Successive cohorts of the elderly have enjoyed better financial conditions than their elderly predecessors, due largely to Social Security, greater accumulated assets, and more widespread pension rights.

When individuals rather than cohorts are followed through the use of panel surveys, however, a different picture emerges. Following individuals from 1968 to 1982, Greg J. Duncan and his associates (1986) found that the family incomes (adjusted for family size) of people over fifty-five years old dropped sharply, while the family incomes of children increased. This pattern makes intuitive sense; as the older group retires, the parents of young children are advancing toward their peak earning years. Retirement nearly always means a drop in income; earnings from work tend to be higher than pension income (Schulz 1988: 26–27). Thus, while older people as a group are doing relatively well, and benefiting substantially from government entitlements and public assistance, older individuals tend to lose ground financially. This downward mobility may lead to feelings of "subjective-relative deprivation" as older people adjust to a lower standard of living, and it is a greater source of political ferment than the "objective deprivation" of people who are poor throughout most of the life cycle (Nelson 1982).

Does it follow that older people tend to be less satisfied with their lives than younger adults? Not necessarily. It may be that older people need less money to maintain their preretirement standard of living. Their nutritional needs, assuming good health, are lower;[2] and they have fewer work-related expenses such as child care, clothing, and transportation. On the other hand, some expenses including health

[2] For this reason, the official poverty line for individuals sixty-five years and older is somewhat lower than for persons under sixty-five (Villers Foundation 1987: 12–13).

care and support services tend to be higher for the elderly, and postretirement income is often insufficient for maintaining preretirement living standards (Schulz 1988: 53–54). Regardless of objective financial conditions, however, most studies of subjective well-being across age groups do not find older people to be less satisfied than younger people.[3]

Many people, old and young alike, perceive the problems of the elderly to be greater than they are, and the impression that most older people live in poverty and misery is still widespread (Light 1985: 59–60; Schulz 1988: 2). Myths about the problems of old age emerged in two surveys conducted by Louis Harris and Associates in 1974 and 1981. Of ten problems listed in 1981,[4] nine were "very serious" problems for fewer than one quarter of elderly respondents (high cost of energy was the exception at 42 percent). Yet majorities of adults thought most of these problems were indeed very serious concerns for older people (National Council on the Aging 1975; 1981). Positive attitudes about retirement, furthermore, have increased since midcentury, along with increases in living standards and pension benefits. Survey respondents in the 1940s and 1950s were overwhelmingly concerned about deprivation during the retirement years; by the 1970s, most were optimistic, both before and after retirement (Schulz 1988: 6, 81).

One major study of several cross-sectional surveys during the 1970s concludes that overall subjective well-being tends to be higher among the elderly than among younger adults. There is, in addition, little difference between retired and still-working older adults (Herzog et al. 1982). Sources of happiness and unhappiness are similar across age groups, with few exceptions; younger adults' happiness is more responsive to conditions in work, education, and marriage, while older people's happiness is more affected by their health. Why do older people appear, in general, to be more satisfied? One reason is that they seem to have fewer daily tensions and burdens; life is less hectic with fewer "major life events." Higher religiosity among older people also seems to be related to greater life satisfaction (Herzog et al. 1982: 42–45).

The authors urge caution in the interpretation of results, however. The data, for one thing, are cross-sectional, and age differences in subjective well-being may be due to cohort effects—differences in life ex-

[3] See Herzog et al. (1982) for an extensive study of subjective well-being.

[4] The ten problems were: not enough money to live on, poor health, loneliness, poor housing, fear of crime, not enough education, not enough job opportunities, not enough medical care, high cost of energy, and transportation.

periences between groups of people born at different times—rather than to life-cycle effects—differences between the elderly and the non-elderly at any point in time. We have already noted, for example, that retirees in the 1970s were more optimistic than retirees in the 1940s and 1950s because the objective conditions of retirement had improved. Second, any subjective attitude is difficult to measure and compare quantitatively. Life satisfaction expressed by older people, for example, may reflect the sheer amount of time they have had to adapt to their communities and lifestyles. Finally, older people may simply be more eager to give socially desirable responses to survey questions (Herzog et al. 1982: 45). One article, for example, cites a finding that "nearly 40 percent of the elderly . . . would be willing to have their own Social Security benefits reduced in order to provide more assistance to the aged who live in poverty" (Lenkowsky 1987: 47). But many of those respondents may find it difficult to tell an interviewer that they would rather maintain their own standard of living than help the poor.

Still, there is plenty of evidence that older people feel no more deprived or unhappy than younger people. If there is any factor more likely to trouble the old than the young, that factor is health. Although most older people do not cite poor health as a serious problem, "it is most likely the actual or potential loss of good health which raises the saliency of this resource for older people" (Herzog et al. 1982: 17). The establishment of Medicare and Medicaid in 1965 reduced significantly the burden of medical care costs for the elderly. However, the growth in health care costs has escalated so rapidly—at twice the rate of inflation in recent years—that today the elderly are paying the same proportion of their annual incomes for medical care out-of-pocket (15 percent) that they paid the year Medicare was enacted (Kosterlitz 1986b: 1255; Villers Foundation 1987: 26). These direct costs to older people include charges not covered by Medicare as well as premiums for supplemental, or "medigap," insurance. It is not only the upper- and middle-income elderly who are affected by high health care costs; older people with family incomes below $10,000 were also paying more than 15 percent of their incomes on medical care in 1981 (Brown 1984: 130).

Medicaid, the program established to cover medical expenses for the poor, is not used by nearly two-thirds of the elderly poor, for two major reasons. First, eligible recipients must be not only poor, but virtually devoid of assets. Second, many eligible persons do not apply, due to the stigma of welfare, the bureaucratic hassles, or the lack of awareness about the program (Villers Foundation 1987: 27).

Perhaps the largest gap in Medicare is its emphasis on acute care services over coverage of chronic health conditions. Acute care costs can be extremely expensive, and coverage is important. Chronic conditions, however, strike mainly the elderly, and have eclipsed acute conditions as the major old-age health problem during the twentieth century. One in four people over age sixty-five, and three in five over eighty-five, need long-term care, which Medicare does not cover. Patients needing long-term care must impoverish themselves before they can apply for Medicaid; for spouses, "the options often come down to poverty or divorce" (Demkovich 1984: 1992).

Congress, during the 1980s, took steps to shift the burden of increasing Medicare costs from beneficiaries to health care providers (Kosterlitz 1986b). The Medicare Catastrophic Health Care Act, passed in 1988, increased Medicare coverage of catastrophic medical costs and prescription drugs—through premium increases and a surcharge based on older people's federal tax liability—but still did not cover long-term care, considered far too costly (Rovner 1987, 1988b). Clearly, government has gone a long way toward helping older Americans with health care costs, although gaps in coverage remain.

Finally, a discussion of the social and economic well-being of older Americans must include the complex question of retirement. Does retirement policy create forced dependence and inactivity, or voluntary leisure and autonomy? Do older workers benefit more from mandatory retirement or from its abolition? The answers have been controversial in theoretical work and in practical application. Public opinion is ambivalent; aging-based interest groups are divided; and public and private sector policies are contradictory in their intentions and results.

Most Americans, it seems, oppose mandatory retirement in principle. Young, middle-aged, and older adults oppose a mandatory retirement age by more than two to one.[5] At the same time, there has been a clear trend among men toward early retirement, at least since the Bureau of Labor Statistics began keeping track in 1948. Between that year and 1985, labor force participation dropped from 47 to 16 percent among men sixty-five years and older; it dropped from 90 to 68 percent among men fifty-five to sixty-four years of age. Women's overall participation in the labor force increased dramatically during the same period, and doubled to 42 percent among women fifty-five to sixty-four years of age, but the participation rate dropped slightly

[5] The data are from the ABC News/*Washington Post* Poll of Public Opinion on Aging, March 1982. See chapter 3.

among women over sixty-five years (Kosterlitz 1986a: 2374; U.S. Bureau of the Census 1975).

Despite widespread opposition to mandatory retirement, most evidence suggests that people are retiring by choice, as soon as feasible economically. It is true that many workers surveyed say they intend to keep working past retirement age, and many retirees say they would still work if they could. But multiple surveys show that very few retirees cite lack of job opportunities as the reason for not working, and very few say they would go back to work if they could afford not to. Longitudinal survey findings, furthermore, indicate that retirement attitudes are volatile, and many people retire shortly after expressing the intention to keep working. Retirees, as long as they are not in dire financial straits, enjoy the increased leisure of the retirement years (Schulz 1988: 81–82).

The two main reasons that workers give for deciding to retire are health and potential retirement income (Schulz 1988: 77–84), and poor health has declined steadily as a reason since the early 1970s. Retirement income, on the other hand, has become more widely available, and at increasingly earlier ages, since midcentury. The nation is wealthier and the standard of living is higher, so that more personal and public resources are available for retirement. Social Security benefits have increased, and since 1961 have been available (at reduced levels) to men sixty-two years of age. Private employer-sponsored pension plans have also increased in number and scope, as have early retirement plans and incentives (Kosterlitz 1986a: 2375).

Retirement may not always be voluntary, however, and the degree of choice involved is hard to determine from surveys and unemployment data. Employers' pressures on workers to retire early may be subtle or hard to prove. Out-of-work people over sixty-two years old may prefer to keep working, but find living on pension benefits easier than looking for a new job (Kosterlitz 1986a: 2376). People naturally differ in their desire to retire at any given age. People in physically demanding or mentally tedious jobs are more likely to opt for early retirement, given the choice. Myths about forced retirement, as Foner and Schwab (1983: 81) have put it, may be propagated by "the relatively privileged" professionals "who write about retirement—reporters, professors, and physicians, for example, all of whom have some degree of control over the pace and direction of their work."

Just as retirement attitudes vary with working conditions, so do the retirement policy positions taken by old-age interest groups vary by group composition. The largely white-collar American Association of Retired Persons, for example, has opposed mandatory retirement and has supported policies to encourage work after age sixty-five. The National Council of Senior Citizens, with its labor union ties, has placed more emphasis on maintaining or raising retirement benefits at earlier ages (Achenbaum 1986: 117; Pratt 1983: 158).

Is flexibility, therefore in both retirement age and income availability, the optimal policy goal for older people? Again, there are differences of opinion. Some maintain that the "flexibility" is an illusion for workers, reality for employers. Flexibility is built into retirement policies in order to regulate the labor force—to increase the labor pool in times of manpower shortages, and constrict it again when younger workers are plentiful. This serves the needs of employers, according to the argument, but not those of employees. Workers would benefit more from a fixed retirement age policy, granting equal rights of retirement to all, and reducing uncertainty for workers. Others, however, contend that a fixed retirement age renders older people dependent upon, and peripheral to, mainstream society. In this view, as well, the interests of employers, and not workers, form the basis of retirement policy (Guillemard 1983: 11–12; Graebner 1980).

The sources and goals of retirement policy may be open to question, but there is no question that retirement has become longer and more financially secure during the twentieth century. It is also clear that older Americans have made substantial economic and political gains during the last few decades. Poverty still plagues millions, and many needs still go unmet, but the elderly in general have benefited from a panoply of government programs and services, as well as private sector initiatives and general economic prosperity.

It does not necessarily follow that they, or the organizations representing them, have been powerful in American politics. The degree of power that aging-based interest groups have wielded in achieving these gains has been a controversial point in the literature, for two major reasons. First, analyses at different points in time can lead to different conclusions. We will see that these groups have become increasingly influential, due to their own growth and to changes in the political environment. Second, other factors are involved in the shaping of policy that affects older people, and it is not easy to sort out the influences. The role of aging-based political organizations cannot be judged merely by the results; the aging policy process must be examined as well.

FACTORS INFLUENCING POLICY

The demands and pressures of organized groups upon policy makers constitute only part of the overall process that results in public policy. The role of organized groups is often exaggerated, or treated in near isolation, in studies such as this one that focus primarily on interest groups in politics. In the analysis to follow, I attempt to look at the role of aging-based interest groups, not only in relation to the whole constellation of interest groups, but also in the larger context of political actors and influences (Hudson and Strate 1985: 567–80; see also Hudson 1980; Myles 1983).

Economic developments and macroeconomic policy affect government social welfare policies toward the elderly and other groups. While interest groups, parties, policy elites and other actors may determine specific policies, the economic context sets the parameters within which specific policies are made. Industrialization and economic growth, for example, generated the resources for increased leisure and a higher standard of living at all stages of the life cycle. Industrial development also increased individual mobility and disrupted traditional familial bonds, shifting much of the care and responsibility for the elderly from the family to the state. Retirement and pension plans arose from the economic need to regulate the labor force. These factors place broad constraints upon political activities within the system.

The political culture, prevailing values, and public opinion are also important elements in the political environment within which interest groups function. Policies that benefit older people, as noted in previous chapters, enjoy overwhelming public support. People recognize the elderly as a legitimate and deserving recipient group; people also recognize their own interests in supporting government benefits for their own elderly family members and their own futures. The social insurance principle—wherein workers contribute now and reap benefits later—is more universally accepted than public assistance programs, which are perceived as government "handouts" to the "undeserving."

Existing policies and programs influence the direction and content of future policies. Incremental adjustments are easier to design, pass, and implement than are wholesale changes in the status quo. This is not to say that policy changes are always small and insignificant, but rather that it is much easier to build onto the programs and bureaucratic structures already in place. To tear down and replace what is already there, on the other hand, is politically and economically impractical if not impossible, with government beneficiaries and administrators defending their turf.

Government officials and policy professionals also play a leading role in policy formation and advocacy. Elected officials often become specialists in a particular policy area and important advocates for certain constituencies. The most prominent crusader for elderly rights in Congress, until his death at the age of eighty-eight in 1989, was Florida

Democrat Claude Pepper. Furthermore, many advocacy groups are formed, or encouraged into action, as a *consequence* of government expansion. Politicians and bureaucrats working in the aging field are naturally interested in mobilizing political support for their own legislation and programs; they are not simply passive recipients of public demands. Government expansion gives both beneficiaries and service providers a stake in the system (Cigler and Loomis 1983: 12–14; Walker 1983: 402).

Within any particular policy system there is usually a variety of active and influential interest groups. These include organizations of the direct beneficiaries—senior citizen organizations in the case of aging policy. They also include allied groups and countervailing groups. Separating the winners from the losers—and from the inconsequentials—is not easy. The influence of a particular group should not be confused either with the intensity of its effort or with the outcome of the policy. Often, groups that worked the hardest or that gained the most in the end, were irrelevant in the actual policy process, or may have even opposed the very policy from which they benefited. Such was the case with the American Medical Association, which opposed Medicare but has since benefited from the resulting inflated medical care costs (Marmor 1973: 113–24).

Finally, broad partisan or ideological alignments may be of greater consequence in a particular policy area than the competition among narrower interest groups. This may depend largely on the scope of the policy. Lowi's (1964) public policy typology helps to illuminate the differences. Lowi distinguishes between *distributive* policies, which parcel out relatively small benefits to specific parties; *regulatory* policies, which govern the relations between groups and institutions; and *redistributive* policies, which dispense resources among broad socioeconomic groups. Redistributive policies are the most far-reaching, and the most likely to involve partisan and ideological battles that go beyond interest group bargain and compromise.

INTEREST GROUPS IN THE AGING POLICY
NETWORK: THE 1960S AND 1970S

Much of the political activity and government expansion during the past quarter of a century have focused on aging. The elderly have become one of the nation's most prominent beneficiary groups. Congress passed Medicare and Medicaid in 1965, and both programs have since received funding increases. The Older Americans Act of 1965 established the Administration on Aging within the Department of Health,

Education and Welfare (now Health and Human Services) as an agency responsible for development and coordination of elderly social services. In 1972, Social Security benefits were expanded and tied to cost of living increases. Supplemental Security Income established a minimum income for the elderly. Social services and funding provided under the Older Americans Act, as well as the role of state and area agencies on aging, were increased in 1973. The 1974 Employee Retirement Income Security Act (ERISA) protected retired workers covered by private pension plans, by establishing minimum legal standards, financial safeguards, and disclosure requirements. Congress expanded housing assistance to the elderly in 1974, abolished mandatory retirement prior to age seventy in 1978, and abolished it altogether—with a few exemptions—in 1986. At the state and local levels, older people have enjoyed such advantages as property and income tax relief, transportation discount fares, and social services.

Structural changes in Congress, the White House, and the federal bureaucracy, in state and local government, in private sector interest groups, and in professional associations and academic institutions all reflect a growing attentiveness to the concerns of old age. Both chambers of Congress for example, had permanent special committees on aging by 1974. In the early 1970s a Federal Council on Aging and a cabinet-level committee on aging were set up to advise the president. The White House Conference on Aging has convened every ten years since 1961 for the purpose of producing aging policy proposals and recommendations. (See also Hudson 1980; Lammers 1983; Pratt 1976; Vinyard 1978, 1973.)

Developments on the interest group scene have been equally lively. Existing old-age organizations, previously more service oriented than politically involved, have expanded their political activity since the early 1960s, and several new aging-based interest groups have emerged. Thousands of membership groups, private foundations, trade associations, service provider organizations, and professional and academic associations have become actively involved in aging advocacy.[6] The diversity of aging advocacy groups reflects the diversity of older Americans themselves—the differences, for example, in their socioeconomic status, activity, independence, occupation, previous and current group loyalties, and political or ideological orientation. Yet the existence and size of these groups, as well as the proliferation of aging-based government programs and benefits, all indicate that the

---

[6] See chapter 2 for a more detailed description of aging-based political organizations. See also Pratt (1983; 1976); Binstock (1972); Peirce and Choharis (1982).

elderly have been firmly established as a distinct group with common interests, needs, and legitimate demands.

Aging policies in the 1960s and 1970s ranged from distributive, positive-sum and low-cost programs, to redistributive, large-scale programs affecting broad socioeconomic population groups. Organizations representing the elderly are potentially in a position to influence both types of policies. They have the political advantages of a narrow interest group, able to build alliances with government officials in specialized policy areas. At the same time, they have the broad appeal of a public interest group whose political fortunes affect everyone, in the future if not the present. The simultaneous emergence and growth of aging-based interest groups and aging programs and benefits might lead to the conclusion that the groups pressured the government for the policies, and won. This interpretation is far from universally accepted, however. The senior organizations in the 1960s and 1970s, by many accounts, played at best a peripheral role, relative to other organizations and political elites in the aging policy system.

Many characteristics of the American political system have militated against the influence of broad constituencies such as the elderly. The relatively decentralized nature of American government facilitates access by smaller and narrower groups (see, e.g., McConnell 1966; McFarland 1983). The federal government is organized, to a large extent, along functional as well as clientele lines—especially when the clients are consumers rather than producers—so that policies and programs of direct concern to the aging are fragmented and not well coordinated. Responsibility for income maintenance, employment, health care, housing assistance, and social services for the elderly lies with several agencies—some twenty-four agencies for more than eighty programs (Estes 1979: 80–81; Lammers 1983: 79; Pratt 1976: 210). Aging policy jurisdiction is likewise parceled out across congressional committees; the special aging committees in both chambers, though permanent, do not have legislative authority. Lobbyists for aging-based interest groups must spread themselves thin if they want to reach all the relevant policy makers, while lobbyists for producer groups or groups with a narrower focus can be correspondingly more concentrated in their approach.

This fragmentation of administrative responsibility, together with a decentralized national legislature, promotes the formation of narrowly focused alliances between congressional committees, agencies, and interest groups, variously known as iron triangles, subgovernments, issue networks, or policy subsystems. Such arrangements tend to favor interest groups composed of producers, service providers, or professionals, over consumer organizations. Hospital and medical associations, for example, historically have wielded tremendous influence in the making of health policy. Other groups enjoying special access include nursing home associations in long-term care policy, builders and real estate developers in housing policy, and gerontological specialists in aging social services policy (Elder and Cobb 1984; Estes 1979; Pratt 1983; Pynoos 1984).

Not all political battles over legislation, of course, are confined to such small, tight policy subsystems. Nor are producer and service provider organizations always triumphant. The politics of the 1960s and 1970s produced some major redistributive policies that eased the financial burdens accompanying retirement and old age—often over the objections of powerful business and professional organizations. The American Medical Association, for example, worked hard for decades to prevent the passage of Medicare. Business associations such as the U.S. Chamber of Commerce opposed many of the private pension regulations comprising the Employee Retirement Income Security Act (ERISA) of 1974.

Yet it was often not the activity of the senior organizations that was decisive; it was, rather, that of their coalitional allies. The aging organizations, according to many observers, played a secondary role at best in achieving the political gains of the 1960s and 1970s, while the activity of allied groups was more influential. Organized labor was especially prominent during this period. Labor initiative and support were critical to the passage of Medicare, ERISA, and improvements in Social Security benefits. In addition, the blind and disabled helped work for expanded Supplemental Security Income benefits; consumer groups pressed for regulation of nursing homes and prescription drugs; social welfare lobbies aided the elderly on a number of programs and benefits (Elder and Cobb 1984: 119; Lammers 1983: 64; Vinyard 1978: 25; Williamson et al. 1982: 11–12).

Political elites in the executive and legislative branches of government have also taken a lead in aging policy innovation. Some contend that policy experts and professionals dominated the most far-reaching and costly policy areas during the sixties and seventies, while the senior membership organizations limited their focus primarily to less costly and controversial services. Accounts of policy making in Medicare (Marmor 1973) and in Social Security (Derthick 1979b) during this period, for example, make almost no mention of the aging-based interest groups, focusing instead on the role of key legislators and administrators with partisan preferences and expertise in the field. The senior organizations, meanwhile, were concentrating their efforts and influence on smaller-scale benefit programs, such as the Older Americans Act, which provide some symbolic concessions—an office set up to "coordinate" government programs for the aging, for example—and relatively small in-kind benefits and social services (Binstock 1972; Hudson and Strate 1985: 571–76; Vinyard 1983: 182–93).

Not everyone, of course, thought the activities of the aging-based organizations were irrelevant to the political gains of this period. Some observers credit these groups with generating the pressure that proved decisive. In Pratt's (1976) account of the battle for the Social Security amendments of 1972, for example, the National Council of Senior Citizens in particular played a major role. The 1972 amendments, which raised Social Security benefits by 20 percent, raised the tax base, and authorized the automatic cost-of-living adjustment, represent some of the most far-reaching economic advances for older people since Social Security's initial passage in 1935. Economic and political conditions favored these changes; powerful congressional leaders Wilbur Mills and Frank Church were among the sponsors, and there was a surplus in the Social Security trust fund. "But had NCSC, or some like-minded group with similar resources not intervened, the legislative result would almost certainly have been different" (Pratt 1976: 149).

Nevertheless, even the scholars who acknowledge the influence of the senior organizations upon aging policy in the 1960s and 1970s—including Pratt—are restrained in their enthusiasm. The influence of senior organizations was generally overshadowed by that of other groups and individuals (Pratt 1983: 164–78). Most would agree with Williamson, Evans, and Powell, that most events of the period "interpreted as major victories for the aged, are largely the product of efforts of others on behalf of the aged, rather than being due to the political influence of the elderly themselves" (Williamson et al. 1982: 12).

Analysts have offered two main reasons for the relatively marginal role played by senior organizations in the political advances of the 1960s and 1970s. First, the aging-based organizations that existed during this period were still too inward-looking, preoccupied with attracting members, and busy establishing organizational stability, to engage heavily in political advocacy (Pratt 1982, 1983). Many of the groups, in fact, either emerged or became politically active *after* much of the pathbreaking legislation—Medicare, Medicaid, and the Older Americans Act, for example—had been passed. Aging group leaders and members became more aware of government benefits for the elderly once those benefits were in place. "Most groups formed during this period," as Walker has observed (1983: 403), "did not force their way in from outside the system; they were brought into being at the bidding of the patrons themselves in a form of political mobilization from the top down." Older people, like many disadvantaged groups, have been moved to political action not so much by absolute misery, but by rising expectations.

The other reason cited for the aging-based groups' marginal role during this period is their middle-class bias and lack of attention to issues targeted at the poorest of the elderly, such as Supplemental Security Income and Medicaid. This limited their involvement in policies with the greatest potential for redistribution of resources to the most disadvantaged. The senior organizations directed their energies instead to piecemeal programs designed to alleviate the "problem" of old age and to help individuals who had "failed" to save enough to carry themselves through the final decades of their lives (Binstock 1972; Hudson and Strate 1985: 573–74; Estes 1983, 1979: 222–30). An interest group may have "power" over limited resources and marginal policy areas, without having the power to produce the political and economic changes that would substantially improve many people's lives.

THE GROWING INFLUENCE OF OLD-AGE POLITICAL ORGANIZATIONS

There is still no consensus, either in the literature or among policy makers, on how much influence the senior organizations have. But their reputation is growing. By the early 1980s, many observers were more sanguine about the ability of these organizations to influence even broad, redistributive policies, and to provide a more effective countervailing force to opposing groups. Now they were hailed as potent lobbyists in aging politics and on general human services issues (e.g. Peirce and Choharis 1982; Pratt 1982). Among interviewees active in the aging policy area—in both executive agencies and congressional committee staffs—the conclusion was nearly unanimous in 1985 and 1986: The elderly, as represented by their organizations, had become their own best advocates.

What led to the change? Most interviewees, as we will see in the following section, cited two major organizational resources which the aging-based groups had developed to great advantage: their mass constituency, and their policy expertise. In addition, the growth and maturity of the senior organizations after the mid-1960s reflected a general trend in American politics: the rise of citizen groups— organizations not based on commercial interests or occupational categories (Walker 1983; Cigler and Loomis 1986). Aging-based interest groups benefited from the same conditions that encouraged the growth and influence of citizen groups in general.

The proliferation of "citizen" and "public interest" groups has received a good deal of attention during the last decade.[7] While many of these groups are small "staff organizations" claiming to represent broad public or consumer interests, the number of mass membership groups has grown as well. There are several possible reasons for the proliferation of these groups. Some have pointed to the weakening of political parties and party organization, leaving other political organizations to fill the gap (Berry 1984; Cigler and Loomis 1986; McFarland 1984; Wilson 1981). Demographic, technological, and attitudinal changes have also had an impact. The population has become more affluent and more educated, both characteristics related to political participation. The growth of communications technologies such as WATS lines and computerized mailing lists has enhanced the ability of organizations to generate mass appeals. Finally, rising public expectations of government coupled with public skepticism toward major institutions, evident in public opinion polls, increase the attractiveness of organizational appeals (Berry 1984, 1977; Moe 1981; Wilson 1981).

The new citizen organizations have been overwhelmingly middle-class; it is not the most disadvantaged who are likely to form and join political organizations. The aging-based organizations are no exception. Older people as a group may be considered disadvantaged in some respects; they are often victims of age discrimination, the financial hardships of a fixed income, dependence on government programs, and rising medical costs. A disproportionate number of the elderly still live near or below the poverty line. However, those who join the senior organizations tend to be relatively well off. Many carry the political skills and contacts developed during their years in business or government, and in retirement they enjoy the leisure time to engage in political activity (Peirce and Choharis 1982).

A related change in the political system affecting interest group activity has been the decline of tight interest group–congressional committee–administrative agency alliances, the iron triangles, that have dominated many policy areas. These alliances, in which narrowly fo-

---

[7] A public interest group is "one that seeks a collective good, the achievement of which will not selectively or materially benefit the membership or activists of the organization" (Berry 1977: 7).

cused interest groups tend to be the dominant private sector participants, seem to be giving way to more fluid, permeable "issue networks." These issue networks are more accessible to a larger number
of actors and broad-based organizations. They are also more conducive to the formation of ad hoc coalitions of groups around specific
issues (Gais et al. 1984; Salisbury 1983: 368).

This is a significant change for the aging-based interest groups in
their dealings with the fragmented aging policy system. Now these
groups are better able to shift attention from one issue area to another,
and to wield greater influence on issues formerly dominated by narrow
or specialized interest groups. Social Security, for example, was largely
under the control of an autonomous policy elite for many years, but
has recently become more open to the scrutiny of a wider array of
participants (Derthick 1979a). In housing policy, to cite another example, AARP and NCSC have just begun to take an active role in an area
that until recently attracted little interest group activity beyond that of
provider groups and housing officials (Pynoos 1984). Coalition building is easier, too, as illustrated by Save Our Security—a coalition of
senior, liberal, and labor organizations fighting Social Security cutbacks—which played a major role in opposing the Reagan administration's proposed Social Security cutbacks in 1981.

The fluidity of issue networks has not gone unnoticed by people in
the aging field in Washington. In his 1976 book, *The Gray Lobby*,
Henry Pratt identified three major separate subsystems within the aging policy system, and listed the principal congressional committees
and subcommittees, executive agencies, and interest groups involved
in each. Since the mid-1970s, according to interviewees who have
worked in the aging field for several years, the distinctions between
these three subsystems—income and health maintenance, social services, and manpower and employment—have diminished and blurred.
The issue of long-term care, for example, is becoming a major focus
for actors both in income and health maintenance and in social services; and manpower and employment issues are increasingly tied to
changes in Social Security, such as age of eligibility and taxation of
benefits. Congressional committee jurisdiction in these areas is less
clear-cut than a decade ago, particularly in the Senate, which tends to
be less rule-bound and rigidly structured than the House. While the
aging policy system remains fragmented, there now seems to be more
overlap between subsystems. This trend represents an advantage for
broad consumer groups in some of the policy domains formerly dominated by narrower producer and service provider groups.

GROWING INFLUENCE OF INTEREST GROUPS
IN THE AGING POLICY NETWORK

The aging-based political organizations in the last decade have not merely been swept along in the wake of citizen group expansion; they have now become leaders in organizational growth and diversity. At a time when many mass-based citizen groups are beginning to decline in membership and resources after having peaked in the 1970s (Salisbury 1983: 363–65), the American Association of Retired Persons continues to grow by millions of members annually, and the other aging-based groups are expanding or holding steady. These organizations have developed techniques for constituency mobilization at the national and local levels, as well as subject expertise in aging policy issues, and policy makers appreciate and sometimes fear these qualities.

The aging-based organizations have huge memberships, as well as the means for spurring their members to action on specific issues. Although many members join for purposes other than political participation, and although many may not be politically active on a regular basis, they often respond *en masse* to calls for action by the leadership. The American Association of Retired Persons (AARP) and the National Committee to Preserve Social Security and Medicare (NCPSSM), in particular, generate massive letter-writing, petition, and telephone campaigns at short notice. Congressional staff members, in a recent survey, cited senior political organizations as "the most successful group in mobilizing grass roots support for their positions" (Fowler and Shaiko 1987: 4).

Organizations with networks of local chapters and affiliates, like the National Council of Senior Citizens (NCSC), the Gray Panthers, and AARP, can draw large turnouts at local meetings, candidate forums, and local and national demonstrations. All of the senior groups publicize aging issues widely at election time, pressuring individual members of Congress. Although politicians realize that the elderly are far from a unified voting bloc, they also fear the impact of a district-wide pre-election voter educational effort by organized groups. The ability to use the "electoral bluff" (Binstock 1972) has become a more important source of group influence with the partisan decline of recent decades. Politicians have become more attentive than before to the election-oriented activities of mass membership organizations that work independently of political party organizations (Lammers 1981: 286).

The aging-based organizations have shifted increasingly from service-oriented activities to political education and activism. Some interviewees in government believe this shift arises from rank-and-file pressure as well as—perhaps more than—from leadership initiative. The elderly, they insist, have become more aware of the issues affecting them, more vocal and more politicized. It is true that older people are increasingly well-educated and affluent, and enjoy more leisure time than ever—all conducive to political activity. On the other hand, most older people are not particularly concerned about aging policy issues, according to survey evidence presented in chapter three. The senior organizations, it appears from the interviews, have effectively portrayed the elderly as a politically conscious and active sector, prepared to support or obstruct a politician's ambitions based on his or her old-age policy record.

President Reagan discovered the power of the aging constituency in 1981, when he was forced to withdraw his proposals for drastic cuts in Social Security retirement and disability benefits. The president subsequently created the National Commission on Social Security Reform to defuse the issue, and to make recommendations on how to restore the Social Security trust fund surplus. The negotiations that led to the 1983 Social Security amendments were highly partisan; the key decision makers were top-level administration officials and congressional leaders; and the aging-based and other interest groups involved all made substantial concessions (Light 1985).

Still, the senior organizations—including the newly formed National Committee to Preserve Social Security and Medicare in addition to the more established groups—continued to flood the Capitol and the White House with constituency mail opposing Social Security benefit cuts. Members of Congress do not dare offend the elderly; any current or future benefit cuts, one staff member asserted, have to be "buried in package bills" to decrease their visibility. In the 1984 debates against challenger Walter Mondale, the president could not emphasize strongly enough his promise not to cut Social Security. Even "after the Reagan Revolution made its challenge" to cut domestic spending, according to Reagan's former budget director, David Stockman, "Congress will not take on the 36 million who get the social insurance checks" (Stockman 1987:197). It is evident from interviews with policy makers that the letter-writing and telephone campaigns, meetings, and demonstrations sponsored by old-age political organizations have been instrumental in building the formidable political reputation of the elderly.

Employees of the legislative branch are generally more impressed than those of the executive branch with the organizations' membership size and participation. The pressure exerted by mass constituency mobilization is most effective in dealing with elected officials, and more effective at the formation and advocacy stages of policy making than at the implementation stage. Organization members can be moved to respond to upcoming legislative action, particularly if it threatens existing programs and benefits, as in the case of the proposed Social Security cuts in 1981. Administrators in the executive branch, on the other hand, are less impressed. They either do not mention constituency pressure at all, or they refer to it as "simplistic," "predictable," and "uncompromising." Caught up in the details of policy implementation and working with state and local levels of government, agency officials are more attuned to the influence of government associations, such as the National Association of Counties, the National Association of State Units on Aging, and the National Association of Area Agencies on Aging.

Partisanship also influences policy makers' attitudes toward aging-based interest groups, and partially accounts for the differences in opinion between legislators and executive branch administrators. Most agency officials interviewed were Republican administration appointees, committed to domestic spending reductions, and therefore less sympathetic to elderly organizations' demands. Some of the aging organization staff people believe that the Administration on Aging and the Federal Council on Aging (a presidential advisory council) have "sunk" into the "bureaucratic quagmire" under the Reagan administration, reducing their role as aging advocates within the government.

Still, policy makers in both the executive and legislative branches of government are impressed by the other major resource of modern aging-based organizations: their policy expertise. While their mass actions draw attention to aging problems, their policy analysts produce detailed and sophisticated solutions; the pragmatism of the latter balances the stridency of the former. These organizations—in particular, the American Association of Retired Persons, the National Council of Senior Citizens, the National Council on the Aging, and the Villers Foundation—engage lobbyists and analysts in their Washington offices who are well known and respected among policy makers of both parties. There is, in fact, much circulation of staff personnel between government and the elderly associations. It is the ability to offer facts, expert testimony at hearings, and workable solutions and compromises, that gives these groups their power and their access to decision makers, according to congressional aides. Their expertise not only helps to sway the undecided, but also to bolster the efforts of advocates within Congress. Activist policy makers can take advantage of the organizations' information and ideas to help persuade congressional colleagues and push their own legislative agenda. This was the advocacy role played by the late Claude Pepper.

The growing influence of the aging-based organizations is nowhere more evident than in the field of health care legislation. Health care is a broad policy area affecting many groups and absorbing a massive share of the federal budget. When Medicare and Medicaid became law in 1965, many analysts considered the influence of senior organizations to be relatively marginal, despite the fact that the elderly were among the most prominent beneficiaries of those programs (Marmor 1973). The aging-based groups that existed at the time were still young; NCSC was still dominated by its parent organization, the AFL-CIO, and AARP was still more service oriented than politically active.

Today, the elderly organizations have made health care quality and cost containment among their top priorities, and virtually every account of health care politics features these groups prominently. Professional health care associations such as the American Medical Association and the American Hospital Association—which opposed Medicare—are still powerful, as they were then. But, as one health care administrator put it, the senior organizations today present a "very effective countervailing force" to the professional medical groups, which before the 1970s had "no effective opposition" among interest groups. When Congress sought ways to cut Medicare in the early 1980s, for example, staff analysts in AARP and NCSC were instrumental in deflecting some of the costs to doctors and hospitals after gathering data on the growing medical expenses faced by elderly individuals.

Currently, two of the major domestic policy issues being debated in Washington are Medicare expansion and long-term care. Senior organizations have taken a leading role in the politics surrounding both issues, and their activities illustrate the differences in tactics and strategies, as well as in views, among the various old-age groups.

The Medicare Catastrophic Health Care Act of 1988 was the largest expansion of Medicare coverage since the program's inception, adding more complete coverage of acute care and prescription drug expenses. Funding for the added coverage came from Medicare premium increases and an income tax surcharge on the elderly; it was paid for, in other words, by Medicare beneficiaries themselves. This law provided a good illustration of how interest groups and legislators interact in the legislative process. It also dramatized the policy disagreements among aging-based groups—not disagreements over the expanded coverage, but over the method of funding.

By all accounts AARP was the leading interest group advocate of the bill, and NCSC was also a prominent supporter (e.g., Rovner 1987,

1988a; Kosterlitz 1987a). Both organizations helped supporters of the bill in Congress by researching the health care needs of older people and possible solutions, devising compromise positions, and testifying at hearings. AARP's efforts were effective despite opposition to the Medicare premium increases and the income tax surcharge from many AARP members. The fact that congressional supporters publicly and repeatedly cited AARP and NCSC as advocates of the bill, in order to claim that they had the backing of important groups in the private sector, illustrates the prestige of AARP and NCSC among policy makers. The bill's advocates were successful even in the face of opposition from such powerful producer groups as the Pharmaceutical Manufacturers Association.

Producer groups were not the only opponents of the Medicare Catastrophic Health Care bill; strident opposition came also from the ranks of the old-age organizations themselves. Both NCPSSM and the Gray Panthers opposed the legislation on two grounds: the elderly themselves paid for the expanded coverage, and coverage did not extend to long-term care for chronic illness. NCPSSM was the most visible opponent among old-age groups in Washington; once again the group used urgent messages in mass mailings and newsletters to whip up elderly opposition to the bill. The group's opposition, however, was disparaged by the bill's supporters in Congress as an irritant. Moreover, congressional opponents of the bill did not appear to consider NCPSSM as a private sector ally. NASC, in all likelihood, opposed the bill as part of its philosophy of disdaining government social welfare spending in general; however, its stand on the issue seems to have gone unnoticed on Capitol Hill.

Most of the old-age political organizations have been more unified on the issue of long-term care. Long-term care legislation debated recently in Congress—known as the "Pepper bill" after its main sponsor, Claude Pepper—would provide long-term home health care for all Americans, of all ages, with chronic illnesses. The care would be financed by eliminating the cap on income subject to the 1.45 percent Medicare payroll tax (Rovner 1988b). The lack of a long-term care provision in the Medicare Catastrophic Health Care Act was a major reason for the Gray Panthers' and NCPSSM's resistance to the bill; thus they favor the Pepper bill.

The biggest boost for the Pepper bill from interest groups, however, probably comes from the alliance of AARP and the Villers Foundation. Together, AARP and Villers have conducted research and public opinion polls, and have provided expert information and testimony in support of long-term care legislation. The AARP-Villers alliance combines the gray lobby's most powerful resources: well connected and respected lobbyists from both organizations, and AARP's enormous membership base. Long-term care is a major problem for the elderly poor, and many nonpoor older people needing long-term care have had to impoverish themselves in order to receive it through the Medicaid program. The Pepper bill would tax the affluent in order to pay for long-term care. Thus, the issue is a natural for the Villers Foundation, which focuses on issues affecting the low-income elderly. "Villers is a groundbreaker in supporting means testing and benefits for the elderly poor," said one interviewee—a sentiment echoed by several policy makers. At this writing, it is too early to tell whether the death in 1989 of Representative Pepper will halt progress on the Pepper bill. Complaints from elderly constituents about the premium increase and income surtax in the Medicare Catastrophic Health Care Act pushed Congress to repeal that law in 1989, thereby delaying further consideration of long-term care legislation. Long-term care, at any rate, is likely to be one of the major old-age issues facing government for decades to come.

Both Medicare expansion and long-term care (whether handled through Medicare or separately) are major, costly, redistributive policy areas. The old-age political organizations, whether united or divided, have been visible and influential participants in the politics surrounding both issues.

The senior organizations have ceased being marginal players, and have become major partners, in much of their coalition work with nonelderly groups. Their own growth in resources and influence is part of the reason, but not all of it. Many of the groups that were so instrumental in working for the political gains of the aging in the 1960s and early 1970s have since seen their fortunes decline, according to several interviewees. Organized labor was most often mentioned; important allies in the campaigns for Medicare and Social Security improvements, the unions are now seen by many as declining in influence, at least temporarily. In addition, the 1980s has been a decade of domestic budget cuts in an effort to trim the federal budget deficit. Although many groups have suffered spending reductions, "programs that hand people checks—in particular, social security and other programs for the elderly—have done consistently better than others" (Rauch 1987: 125). Spending on the elderly is still more popular with the public than social welfare spending in general. Now many social welfare lobbies look to the aging groups as leaders in the fight against domestic budget slashing.

While congressional and administrative staff personnel are im-

pressed with the senior organizations' policy expertise and mass constituencies, they are less impressed with the organizations' spending.
While the groups have become more adept at fundraising for their political and other activities—through mass communications, business
associations, and private and government grants—and although a few,
notably NCSC and the National Association of Retired Federal Employees (NARFE), have formed political action committees, they are not big
political spenders. Only NCPSSM, with its massive direct-mail campaigns, and NARFE, were singled out by policy makers as major campaign contributors. According to NCPSSM's fact sheet, the group
"ranked as the third largest lobby in the country in terms of expenditures," and the political action committee it sponsors was ranked elev-
enth in revenues in the 1984 election cycle. "It is," according to one
agency staff member, "the only one with any money."

Another advantage that the aging-based groups have enjoyed is the
popularity and legitimacy of the elderly as a welfare group. This, according to many interviewees, is beginning to wane slightly. Until recently, programs and entitlements benefiting the aging were "sacro-
sanct"; few politicians dared to oppose them. Public opinion polls still
show overwhelming support for government spending on older people, and no politician or interest group wants to come across as opposing the elderly. However, spending on the aging must be justified as
never before; needs must be more carefully documented; federal
spending can no longer be taken for granted. "They *have* to be more
active now," said one congressional aide, "and they have to show that
they're backed by their members." "They no longer call all the shots,"
said another. The atmosphere of fiscal conservatism in Washington has
encouraged new countervailing forces in the form of tax reform groups
and right-wing foundations—some with close ties to the Reagan and
Bush administrations—and has "forced" the aging-based organizations to become more active and visible.

FUTURE PROSPECTS FOR INTEREST
GROUP POWER

Despite the recent ill effects of "budget cutting fever," the senior political organizations appear to be flourishing today after decades of
growth. Yet they, too, could diminish in influence, just as they have
benefited from the decline of other interest groups. What are the prospects for their future survival and political success?

One thing is certain: the older population will continue to grow,
both absolutely and relative to the rest of the population, for at least

another century. The old-age organizations' demographic constituency will expand indefinitely. In 1985, about twenty-eight and a half million people in the United States, or 12 percent of the population, were sixty-five years of age and older. That percentage will increase from about 13.8 percent to about 21.2 percent between 2010 and 2030, the years during which the baby boom generation will reach the age of sixty-five. By 2080, the elderly population is projected to reach 23.5 percent—more than seventy-three million people. The number of Americans eighty-five years of age and older will increase even more rapidly: from one in 100 persons in 1985, to over one in twenty by the year 2080 (U.S. Bureau of the Census 1984: 7–8).

It is difficult to project what this will mean for future taxpayers and pension recipients. Such projections involve the calculation of "dependency ratios," as they are usually called: the "numerical relationships between the 'productive' and 'non-productive' or 'dependent' components of a population" (Friedmann and Adamchak 1983: 58). The "aged" dependency ratio—the number of persons sixty-five years of age and older per one hundred persons aged eighteen to sixty-four—will increase from 19.4 in 1985 to around 37 in 2030, and 41.9 in 2080 (U.S. Bureau of the Census 1984: 6). This large increase is central to the arguments of those who warn of a future Social Security crisis. When children under age eighteen are added in, the total dependency ratio increases more slowly, from 62.1 in 1985, to 74.8 in 2030 and 78.1 in 2080 (U.S. Bureau of the Census 1984: 6).

These dependency ratios based on age groups, however, do not capture the complexity of the labor market. The ratio of workers to nonworkers depends not only on the number of children and elderly, but also on the number of nonworking spouses, unemployed workers, severely disabled persons, and others who are not in the labor force. Projections of dependency ratios that take all these factors into account, of course, are subject to a variety of errors, depending on the assumptions and number of variables used. Friedmann and Adamchak's detailed analysis, for example, projects a *decline* in the total labor force dependency ratio between 1990 and 2050, from 103.2 to 85.5 (1983: 60–64; see also Schulz 1988: 10–13; Myles 1984: 171). Thus, alarmists about the future of Social Security, and about the potential economic burden of an expanding older population, may have a point but it is hard to predict.

Whatever the economic and demographic realities shaping the politics of the twenty-first century, older people are likely to be politically active. They are, as noted earlier, increasingly educated, healthy, long-lived, and responsive to political appeals. They are also increasingly diverse, but so are the aging-based organizations that represent them, and these organizations are masterful in their use of numerous incentives and mass communications technologies to attract members. These various organizations have shown an ability to work together on many old-age issues. They face little public opposition. Not only are Social Security and Medicare popular, but over two-thirds of Americans surveyed recently expressed a willingness to pay higher taxes for "a federal program of long-term care for everyone over 65."[8]

But even if the survival of the aging-based organizations is assured, what about their political power? Most interviewees stressed that the influence of the senior organizations lay in their ability to defend existing old-age programs and benefits, now that they have so much to defend. They are more pragmatic in their politics than they were in the 1960s, and are considered now to be Washington insiders (Pratt 1982; Vinyard 1983: 195). It is easier for an organization to defend the status quo than it is to successfully raise new issues or initiate new policy (Pratt 1983; Wilson 1973: 330). Not only is it easier for a group to veto change than to initiate it, but the existence of government programs creates new allies or patrons within the government itself, as noted earlier (Cigler and Loomis 1983: 12–14; Walker 1983: 403). But some analysts argue that entrenchment and legitimacy within a policy system are not the same as power and influence. The defensiveness of the aging groups may signify a lowering of aspirations and an acceptance of the fact that the needs of many elderly persons—particularly the most disadvantaged—remain unmet (Binstock 1972; Estes 1979).

Now, even the groups' defensive strength is beginning to weaken, as concerns about the federal deficit, and the large share of the budget going to the elderly, are fomenting a political backlash. The elderly, according to several observers, are beginning to lose their status as a group deserving special treatment from the government—at least among political elites if not among the general public (Hudson 1978: 30–32; Williamson et al. 1982: 101). Some public officials, journalists, and scholars are beginning to complain that government benefits based on old age waste funds on affluent older people (Haas 1987; Longman 1985; Rauch 1987; Samuelson 1981). Americans for Generational Equity (AGE) warns that the Social Security system will not be able to support aging baby boomers if it continues supporting "self-sufficient"

[8] Survey undertaken by RL Associates, Princeton, New Jersey, for the American Association of Retired Persons and the Villers Foundation. Reported in the *Presidential Campaign Hotline*, September 22, 1987, item 51.

retirees now. The attitude is spreading that older people have received more than their share from the government, and that limited resources for social welfare should be diverted from the elderly to other needy groups such as families with small children.

COALITIONS AND PARTIES

One major focus of this backlash has been the organizations' perceived failure to lobby in behalf of the poorest and neediest elderly. This type of criticism has come from both sides of the political spectrum: from liberals supportive of social welfare for the disadvantaged, and from conservatives concerned about spending federal dollars to subsidize the middle class. The result has been a broadening of the aging policy agenda, from a major emphasis on universal age-based entitlements, to a larger debate over other appropriate criteria, such as income level, for distributing government aid. The "age versus need" question (Neugarten 1982) has posed a dilemma for both organization leaders and policy makers. Most people in all age groups resist the notion of income-tested or means-tested public assistance, finding it demeaning. However, organizational claims that older people as a group are in need of special treatment from the government are losing credibility.

The debate over the criteria for redistributing resources is part of a larger political trend: the expanding number and types of interest groups active in American politics. Most policy subsystems have become more open and contentious, with more groups participating. Formerly tight and relatively stable iron triangles have given way in many cases to more fluid and shifting issue networks; and temporary coalitions, forming around a single issue and then dissolving, have become common (Cigler and Loomis 1986; Gais et al. 1984). As more groups become involved in the governmental process, they are more likely to challenge the current distribution of resources, and the defense of existing programs becomes more problematic, as it has for the elderly. Cigler and Loomis assert that "many distributive policy areas have been politically redefined as redistributive; . . . the policy agenda is no longer tightly controlled by a narrow group of interests" (1986: 308). Even such a highly legitimate recipient group as the elderly is less immune to challenges from other groups.

The diversity and the legitimacy of the aging-based organizations has helped them meet the challenge with a variety of appeals (see Nelson 1982). They can appeal to the social conscience of policy makers and the public, as the Gray Panthers and the Villers Foundation in particular have done, by emphasizing the needs of the most disadvantaged elderly—the disproportionate number of older people who live near or below the poverty line and who depend on government aid to get by. They can appeal to public sympathy by emphasizing the disadvantages often coinciding with the onset of old age, such as failing health, fixed incomes, and age discrimination in employment. They can appeal to the notion of fairness or social justice on the grounds that older people have earned special treatment after having worked all their lives and contributed their achievements to society (not to mention their Social Security taxes). They can appeal to the public's self-interest by noting that everyone ages, and many have elderly parents and relatives; thus the elderly's gain is everyone's gain. The combination of public relations appeals—for both universal and special benefits, for both rights and needs, for both sympathy and respect—seems to work well for them.

As the diversity of old-age organizations and the backlash against universal old-age benefits have grown, coalitions uniting old-age organizations have diminished in number and influence, while coalitions of elderly and nonelderly groups are becoming more prominent. Generations United is one recent example. In answer to Americans for Generational Equity and other groups opposing universal age-based benefits on the grounds that other needy groups are not getting their share, the National Council on the Aging and the Child Welfare League led the formation of the coalition in 1986. Generations United, with over one hundred organizations representing children and the elderly, supports aid to families and opposes cuts in Social Security. The purpose of the coalition is to discredit the position that gains in some domestic spending programs must lead to cutbacks in others. In this way, the old-age organizations involved—among them, AARP, the Gray Panthers, NCSC, the Older Women's League, organizations representing elderly minorities, and several professional and service provider associations—hope to counter the charge that older people are benefiting from government programs at the expense of children and other groups.

The remaining question is whether interest groups, in the current political environment of shifting coalitions, will become increasingly aligned with political parties. Gais, Peterson, and Walker (1984: 184) suggest that

> a newly centralized, competitive system based upon ideologically consistent political parties is certainly not the only possible future for the American system. It is perhaps more likely that a penetrable,

unpredictable competitive system of conflict resolution will emerge that would frustrate almost all efforts to provide it with national focus and leadership.

They may be correct, as far as aging policy is concerned. Nearly all of the aging-based organizations have carefully avoided partisan politics, emphasizing their bipartisanship.

The leadership of AARP, for example, has carefully avoided any hint of a preference for one party or another. This avoidance of partisanship has extended to its recently inaugurated voter education program, evaluating candidates on the basis of whether they support AARP's positions. AARP's leaders wish neither to offend any group in their broad, diverse membership, nor to sever ties with policy makers of either party.

The Gray Panthers, while certainly not middle-of-the-road in their views, also remain consciously removed from partisan politics. NCPSSM staff members are equally insistent, in organizational publicity pieces and in interviews, that the organization is nonpartisan. Casual observers often assume that NCPSSM is affiliated with the Democratic party, because it was founded by James Roosevelt, oldest son of Franklin D. Roosevelt. The organization, however, has supported candidates of both parties. Policy makers interviewed had very different ideas about NCPSSM's partisan affinities. Some perceived the group as a liberal Democratic ally because of its advocacy of any social insurance expansion. Several others, however, insisted that "they support more Republicans than Democrats," that "they hide their right-wing partisanship behind liberal rhetoric," or that "Roosevelt is a Reaganite."

NASC appears partisan in its views, which correspond with the fiscal conservatism of the Republican party's right wing. However, NASC, too, eschews any overt partisan alliance and claims to be nonpartisan. A spokesman for the organization, in fact, pointed to NASC's alliance with labor and gay rights groups—two traditionally Democratic constituencies—on health issues in California, as evidence of the group's bipartisan activities. The major exception to the old-age organizations' pattern of nonpartisanship is NCSC, which grew out of the Democratic party and maintains ties with organized labor.

Many interest groups in the United States seem to share the attitude that if they align themselves with one party, they will lose political leverage. In the narrow range of interest group politics, organizations feel they can gain the most by playing partisan candidates, and congressional party delegations, against each other, rather than being predictable and consistent in their partisan loyalties. Yet it is macroeconomic policies, not interest group bargaining, that determine the major distribution of resources affecting the elderly, including pension benefits and public health insurance (Myles 1983: 35). And it is political parties, more than interest groups, that set the broad economic agenda. Interest groups may play a significant part in shaping particular distributive or even redistributive policies, as the aging-based groups have done recently in the area of health care. But more broadly, interest groups that remain outside of partisan politics may lose in power what they gain in autonomy.

CHAPTER 6

Who Represents the Elderly?

OLDER Americans are a difficult group to represent. Not only are they deeply divided over the political issues that affect them most directly—such as increases in Social Security, Medicare, and government spending on the elderly in general—but they are apparently no more supportive of such increases—and perhaps even less so—than younger adults. The mass membership organizations of the elderly also vary in their political positions, but most of them lobby consistently for the maintenance and expansion of old-age benefits.

These observations about the political opinions of older Americans, and the political activities of their interest groups, lead to the question of organizational representation. How well do interest groups represent their constituencies? Do interest group leaders' opinions and activities accurately reflect their constituents' interests and desires, or is there a gap between leaders and followers? What do our findings about aging-based interest groups tell us about interest group representation and accountability?

These are not new concerns in the interest group literature. Examples abound of group leaders who differ from the rank and file. Leaders of the women's movement (Zeigler and Poole 1985), the civil rights movement (Lichter 1985), political parties (McClosky 1964), and such organizations as the National Council of Churches, the American Civil Liberties Union, and the AFL–CIO (Schlozman and Tierney 1986: 142; Wilson 1973: 226–27) have been shown to adopt positions contrary to, or more politicized than, those favored by their constituencies.

Twentieth century analysts have pondered the leader-follower separation question at least since Robert Michels' work on the "iron law of oligarchy" appeared in 1915. As large organizations develop bureaucratic structures and institutionalized leadership, according to Michels, the leaders' experience, skills, and greed for power, coupled with the apathy and deference of their followers, result in the dominance of an oligarchy that is largely unresponsive to rank and file preferences. Furthermore, members may often join and remain in organizations for reasons having little to do with any similarity between their opinions and those of the organization leaders, as noted in the literature on exchange and incentive theory and rational choice (e.g., Olson 1965; Salisbury 1969; Weissman 1970; Wilson 1973).

Even more complex and, I would argue, more important than the interaction between leaders and members of formal organizations, is the relationship between group leaders and their purported constituency. Most old-age political organizations claim to speak for, and defend the interests of, all older Americans, not just those who pay membership dues. This type of claim is characteristic not only of aging-based interest groups, but of groups representing many other sectors of society—for example, the civil rights and women's groups and the political parties that were the subjects of the representational studies cited.

Formal organization membership, furthermore, is becoming increasingly difficult to define, with the growth of computerized direct mail techniques. Even the distinction between activist and rank-and-file members (see, e.g., Franke and Dobson 1985) does not capture the complexity. Is a person who writes one check and receives a membership card, for example, as much an organization member as one who attends chapter meetings year after year but neglects to pay dues? It is most important, therefore, to study group representation by examining the interests and views not only of formal organization members, but of the people whom the various organizations claim to represent.

Can we conclude, based on evidence of attitudinal differences between leaders and followers, that interest groups are unrepresentative and unaccountable to their constituents? We cannot; such a conclusion ignores the complexities and nuances of the representative's role. Previous studies of representation have focused primarily on legislatures, but the same concepts may be applied to interest groups as well, both internally and in relation to the polity as a whole. Three points are key to this analysis: (1) Representation is a complicated concept that transcends the simple congruence of opinions between group leaders and followers. (2) An interest group may represent several different constituencies. (3) Interest group representation must be considered in the context of the polity as a whole, which includes other interest groups as well as different representative institutions, each playing a separate but interdependent role.

THE CONCEPT OF REPRESENTATION

Representation, according to De Grazia's (1951: 4) definition, "exists when the characteristics and acts of one vested with public functions are in accord with the desires of one or more persons to whom the functions have objective or subjective importance." This relationship between the actions of the representative and the interests of the represented is the major premise behind all works on political representation. The definition, however, embodies several different ideas about how that relationship is achieved: (1) through resemblance or descriptive similarity between the representative and constituents; (2) through instructions issued by the constituents and carried through by the representative; or (3) through independent actions of the representative on behalf of the constituents (see, e.g., Sartori 1968; Conway 1985: 150–52). It is not, as Pitkin notes, that the meaning of representation is vague; it is, rather, complex and multifaceted, and each use must be studied in context.

The most basic meaning of representation is "a making present of something absent—but not making it literally present. It must be made present indirectly, through an intermediary; it must be made present in some sense, while nevertheless remaining literally absent" (Pitkin 1969: 16). The paradox of representation is that the constituents must participate in some way, in order to select representatives and make their desires known, yet at the same time they must accept their representatives' decisions as legitimate and authoritative (Eulau 1962: 268). They must, in other words, be present and absent simultaneously. Furthermore, direct participation by all in every decision is too cumbersome for effective policy making in a large society; yet both the participation of constituents, and policies that effectively meet their needs, are integral to the concept of representation.

There are many levels of participation and representation in a large society such as the United States—elections, political parties, and interest groups, to name a few—that, in combination, address the various goals of a representative democracy, successfully or unsuccessfully. Most of the relevant literature to date has focused on representative government, with less attention focused on the institutions that represent different interests and views *to* the government. Historical and current controversies over the nature of representative government are relevant to the discussion of interest groups, as we shall see. Interest groups, however, must also be viewed on their own terms as representative institutions. Governments make policy and allocate resources for the society as a whole; interest groups articulate demands and provide a forum for participation, and their scope is usually limited to a sector of society.

One need only survey the ideas of a few major post-Renaissance philosophers in order to get a flavor of the divergent views on representative government.[1] Thomas Hobbes, in the seventeenth century,

---

[1] For a more complete survey of the representation literature, see, e.g., Pitkin (1969;

viewed a representative as one authorized to act on behalf of the citizenry, to rule over the state created to bring order to man's natural chaotic condition. Hobbes's vision emphasized the duties and obligations of citizens to accept authority; the representative is not bound by the wishes of, or accountable to, the represented. Rousseau, a century later, agreed that the representative possessed the authority to act without being held accountable, but he equated representative government to tyranny, incompatible with democracy or the public interest.

Most other views of representation have included some combination of citizen participation and independent action by the representative. John Stuart Mill envisioned the polity as a collection of various interests, each proportionally represented within the government. Citizen participation, in this view, occurs primarily at the local level, on issues affecting their everyday life. The representative's role is mainly that of an *agent*, reflecting accurately the opinions and instructions of those he is chosen to represent. Edmund Burke, on the other hand, viewed the representative more as a *trustee*. His classic statement on the role of legislators in the eighteenth century, while respecting the importance of constituency preferences, defended the representative's responsibility to decide and to act according to his own view of the national interest, even if that view did not coincide exactly with the expressed opinions of his constituents.

Some twentieth century political theorists (e.g., Sartori 1962) have stressed the importance of competing elites and quality of leadership as the basis of representative government. Others (e.g., Pateman 1970) have placed more emphasis on the education and socialization of ordinary citizens to take a more active role in political decisions.

How, then, can we discuss cogently the representativeness of government, or of intermediary organizations, given the wide variety of views on the subject? One convenient distinction, proposed by Eulau (1962: 268–86) for the study of legislatures, but applicable to interest groups as well, is the distinction between the "style" and the "focus" of representation. Style refers to the decision rules guiding a representative's behavior—whether he behaves as an agent, using his constituents' mandate or instructions as a guide; or as a trustee, using his own conscience or evaluations as a guide; or some combination of the two.

The focus of representation refers to the particular group a representative has in mind in making his decisions. In legislative studies, the term usually refers to narrow local interests on the one hand, and

---

1967); Pateman (1970); De Grazia (1951). The following discussion is based primarily on Pitkin (1969).

broad national interests on the other (Eulau 1962: 270). The analog for political organizations might be Punnett's distinction between "sectional" groups and "cause" groups (Punnett 1971: 137). A sectional group is one that attempts to enroll the highest possible percentage of a population sector, and that exists for other purposes besides lobbying the government. A cause group exists specifically to influence government; it lacks the breadth of a sectional group but enjoys more "unity of purpose." Neither type of group exists in pure form, but most tend toward one type or the other.

Interest group leaders may in fact focus on several different constituencies. Aging-based interest groups, for example, may think of their primary focus as older people in general, or a particular subgroup of the elderly, or their own dues-paying members, or a foundation or other major funding source for the organization, or the adherents of a particular class or ideology, or the society as a whole. All of these, as we will see, have served as at least one focus for at least one elderly organization.

Different styles are not, of course, mutually exclusive, and neither are different foci; they may be present simultaneously in a representative's decision. Each style and each focus may serve as a normative basis for any decision on the part of the leadership—and for philosophical views on the nature of representation, as we have seen. The style-focus distinction also can be used in the empirical study of interest groups. The question posed at the beginning of this chapter—Is there a gap between interest group leaders and followers?—is not a simple one, and cannot be answered merely by comparing constituent opinion surveys with leadership decisions. The question is not, Are interest groups representative?—but rather, What are the different ways in which interest groups represent citizen interests and opinions to the government?

In the sections that follow I will discuss the size and breadth, and the participatory and decision making processes, of interest groups in light of representative focus and style. I will then apply the discussion to findings about aging-based interest groups in particular. Finally, I will consider the representative role of interest groups in the polity as a whole.

MEMBERSHIP SIZE AND REPRESENTATIVE FOCUS

Which is more representative, a large interest group or a small one? It is intuitively appealing, on the one hand, to suppose that a larger group with a broader base is more representative, because more people within the sector being represented have a say in the group's decisions. As one analyst put it, "the better an organization is at finding and retaining members, the better it will be able to represent its constituents' interests" (Berry 1984: 67). On the other hand, it also seems logical to suppose that a smaller group is more representative, because its members are more likely to agree with each other—to have "preference homogeneity" (Franke and Dobson 1985)— so that the group's decisions are agreeable to everyone in the group, not just to the majority or to an outspoken minority. But infinite regression in the former case leads to the conclusion that the most representative group is the one that includes everyone—nobody's opinions are left out. And infinite regression in the second case leads to the conclusion that the most representative group is one with a single member; he will always agree with himself. This is to confuse representativeness with numbers in the first case, and with preference homogeneity in the second case.

The size of an organization is not an indicator of the degree of representativeness. It is, rather, an indicator of the *focus* of representation. The focus, in turn, influences the types of incentives an organization will use to attract members, and the types of resources it will use to influence policy. A sectional group, focusing on a broad sector of the population, will use a combination of incentives aimed at maximizing the number of members, and usually including material and/or solidary incentives having little to do with the political goals of the group. It can then use its large membership as a lobbying resource, mobilizing, for example, large letter-writing or electoral campaigns, or political endorsements backed up by a large membership base. A cause group, focusing on a more narrow, issue-oriented or ideological constituency, will be more concerned with attracting dedicated volunteers than with signing up a large, inactive membership. Such a group will emphasize purposive incentives, and stress expertise, financial contributions, and media attention over numbers as political resources.

Group leaders relying on outside sources of funding, such as foundation grants, philanthropists, or government agencies, often do so because their representative focus is a group that is difficult to mobilize politically. Economically disadvantaged groups are particularly difficult to mobilize. Thus, organizations focusing on disadvantaged groups will generally have a hard time subsisting on membership dues. Instead, they must either offer selective incentives of high immediate value, to balance the cost of group participation when personal economic problems are more pressing; or they must rely on other sources of income and resources.

Is a large group with a politically committed membership more representative than a group that attracts members with incentives having little to do with its political goals, or a group that attracts resources by meeting the requirements of a foundation or other funding source? Not necessarily. It is, as we have seen, a matter of representative focus, not a matter of degree of representation.

PARTICIPATION AND REPRESENTATIVE STYLE

Every membership organization must contend with the tension between hierarchy and democratic participation, in its effort to fulfill both of its representational roles: effective advocacy and maximum participation. A related dilemma is that between organizational maintenance and goal achievement; organization leaders must please their members if the group is to survive, and they must also interact with policy makers, making the contacts and the compromises necessary to achieve their policy goals (Freeman 1975: 145–46; Wilson 1973: 313). The tension between hierarchy and participation lies at the heart of representative style: the degree to which a representative uses his own judgment or his constituents' mandate to guide his decisions.

Participation and advocacy are not, of course, polar opposites; success in one endeavor may boost the success of another. Leaders who can boast of political achievements and governmental access are likely to impress their members and attract new ones. Leaders who can claim a large and active following can enhance their credibility and effectiveness with policy makers, and they also benefit from the organizational work of active volunteers. The tension remains, however; as Freeman (1975: 100) notes, "the tightly organized, hierarchical structures necessary to change social institutions conflict directly with the participatory style necessary to maintain membership support and the democratic nature of the movement's goals." Most voluntary organizations, therefore, try to strike a balance between hierarchy and democratic participation; few have either a purely vertical or purely horizontal structure.

The ways in which an organization elicits, and makes use of, member participation determine its representative style. The degree to which organization leaders act as agents or trustees depends both on the opportunities for participation offered by the leaders, and on the ability and willingness of members to participate in organizational decision making. Members of an organization, like citizens of a representative government, may participate in organizational decisions directly, through communication and interaction with the leaders, or indirectly, by choosing the leaders who then make the decisions. Indirect participation is, of course, facilitated by elections in which competing candidates vie for members' votes. But how do organizations encourage (or discourage) direct participation?

One way is through dissemination of information. Membership in a political organization is, in itself, often a motivation for participation in group activities. All of the aging-based mass membership organizations send newsletters to their members on a regular basis, containing political reports, accounts of the group's lobbying activities, and, often, leaders' requests for action by the membership. This information serves to increase political awareness and group consciousness (Cutler 1981: 154; Franke and Dobson 1985: 229).

Another aspect of direct participation is the opportunity for face-to-face interaction with other organization members (Hayes 1986). National organizations that have a network of local chapters offer their members an opportunity to meet with others, to discuss common political issues, increase their awareness, learn more about the leadership, and communicate their opinions. Face-to-face interaction promotes political activity through education and peer pressure, and offers an avenue of indirect communication with national leaders, by way of local intermediaries.

Today, however, it is increasingly common for national organizations to operate out of a central office with few or no local chapters. Organization leaders and staff send out mass appeals for donations, dues, and political actions such as letters to Congress on an upcoming bill. Members respond with a signature and a check, becoming "checkbook" members (Hayes 1986), and forgoing personal interaction with fellow members. This is easier for organization leaders than developing a network of local chapters; it also requires less time and effort on the part of constituents. At the same time, participation of this type tends to be more passive, or reactive, than participation through personal interaction at the local level. The representative style of these organizations tends to be that of the trustee: decisions are made at the national level with little decision making input by most members.

Another aspect of participation and representation differentiates interest groups from governments: members can exit from voluntary organizations, or "vote with their feet," if they are unhappy with the leaders' decisions and activities (Hirschman 1970; Hardin 1982: 73). The option to exit reduces the importance of procedural democracy, whether direct or indirect, in voluntary organizations (Berry 1984: 94–95; Schlozman and Tierney 1986: 134). The option to exit mitigates the organizational tendency to oligarchy discussed by Michels; organizations dependent upon membership support must please their members or lose them. Oligarchy is therefore a more serious hindrance to representative government—from which citizens cannot exit, short of renouncing their citizenship and emigrating—than it is to representation by voluntary organizations.

How important for representation is active participation by the rank and file? This is a point of contention in the literature. If success in meeting the needs of constituents is important to the concept of representation, then quality of leadership may be more important than maximum participation by constituents, who are often apathetic or ill-informed (Sartori 1962). Even when citizen participation is a policy goal, active participation is often left to an "elite group of activists under the general leadership of professional organizers," as in the case of the 1960s War on Poverty (Gilbert 1970: 172–72). Furthermore, constituency participation has sometimes produced delay, divisiveness, and watered-down solutions (Binstock et al. 1985: 604), where hierarchy and centralized decision making might have promoted innovation and rapid results.

Participation, on the other hand, may be important to group effectiveness as well as being a goal in itself. Constituents learn political skills and procedures through participation; they learn how their own personal needs may be addressed collectively. They are able then to communicate their needs to organization leaders and to judge their leaders' performance (Pateman 1970). Even representatives who act as trustees, acting on their own judgment rather than on constituency instructions, will have an easier time of it if constituents' needs can somehow be communicated upward. Participation helps keep representatives of any style informed.

Organization leaders who promote active participation in decision making by the rank and file display the representative style of an agent, acting largely according to constituency mandate. Organization leaders who promote "checkbook memberships"—emphasizing large memberships and centralized decision making with little rank-and-file input—display the representative style of a trustee, acting primarily according to their own judgment. Some organization leaders combine the two styles, establishing active local chapters for rank and file input and activity, and signing up larger numbers of less active members through mass mailings. None of these types of organizations can be said to be "more representative" than the others; it is a matter of representative style.

REPRESENTATION IN AGING-BASED ORGANIZATIONS

Organizations for older people in the United States vary widely in representative focus and style. Yet the question of leader-follower separation remains relevant; the representational variety cannot be interpreted to mean that any organization is representative of its constituency. Such a conclusion renders the concept of representation meaningless, if nothing can be excluded from the definition. Are older people represented by their interest groups? The answer to this question lies in the answers to two others: Are older people represented *falsely* by their interest groups? Are some older people *excluded* from representation by their interest groups? Organization leaders and policy makers have their own answers to these questions, expressed in interviews and in organizational brochures and public releases.

Representative Focus

Most aging-based organizations claim to represent all older people—a politically astute claim, since "narrow special interests" have received so much bad press, and since the elderly are still a popular and legitimate recipient group. It is clear, nevertheless, that each organization has a different focus, overlapping in many cases, but different. The diversity of groups, we have noted earlier, reflects but does not match the diversity of older people themselves.

Aging policy itself reflects two complementary but competing goals: adequacy and equity. The adequacy goal seeks to protect the most needy by assuring a minimum standard of living and granting special benefits to the disadvantaged. The equity goal seeks to reward individualism and self-reliance by basing government benefits on the amount contributed individually during the working years (Achenbaum 1986: 2). In addition, the equity issue must address the needs of both the downwardly mobile elderly who draw less income after retirement, and the affluent elderly (Nelson 1982).

These distinct policy goals have created two major dilemmas for aging-based organizations, dilemmas recognized by both policy makers and group leaders. One is whether to support universal benefits for all older people—inviting cries of "budget-busting"—or to support highly unpopular means-tested benefits for the poor and disadvantaged elderly. The other dilemma is whether to project an image of older people as generally needy—promoting sympathy but also stigmatizing old age—or to project the elderly as vital, energetic assets to society, thereby prompting others to ask why they would need government aid in the first place.

The representative focus of elderly organizations ranges from the broad and inclusive, to the narrowly defined and exclusive. The major groups of older people targeted by organizations are demographic and ideological subgroups. The most inclusive organization is the American Association of Retired Persons (AARP), open to anyone age fifty or over, and numbering over twenty-eight million members. AARP is, according to its own fact sheet, "a nonprofit, nonpartisan organization dedicated to helping older Americans achieve retirement lives of independence, dignity and purpose"; its lobbyists "represent the interests of all older Americans." AARP has been known for many years as an organization of middle- to upper-middle-class professionals and executives whose major issue was the elimination of mandatory retirement. In the last few years, AARP has increased its efforts to recruit minority members and to lobby for social spending on the disadvantaged; women's and minority affairs are two of its four current top priorities, along with health care and worker equity. However, it continues to emphasize equity issues, opposing the imposition of income tests—based on personal income—or means tests—based on assets as well as income—upon Social Security benefits.

The relatively new National Committee to Preserve Social Security and Medicare (NCPSSM) is also broad in its membership focus, though narrower in its issue focus. NCPSSM claims to be a bipartisan "grassroots lobby" of "senior citizens and other concerned Americans," although it targets primarily older people. The group focuses on social insurance programs, firmly opposing means or income testing of Social Security and Medicare. The National Council of Senior Citizens (NCSC) also promotes broad-based grassroots activity, but is more focused on low-income needs and targeted social programs as well as universal Social Security and Medicare benefits.

The two organizations with the sharpest ideological focus are the Gray Panthers on the Left and the National Alliance of Senior Citizens (NASC) on the Right. Both naturally claim to support policies for the benefit of all older people as well as of the general public but both recognize the confines of their constituencies and the limits of their appeal. NASC touts itself as "the national organization for responsible seniors," opposing federal aid programs and strongly promoting policy goals of equity over adequacy. NASC also promotes strong national security and domestic crime control. The Gray Panthers organization, at the other end of the spectrum, promotes income redistribution and social services for the most needy, as well as peace and demilitarization issues.

Other mass membership aging-based organizations do not limit their focus by issue or ideology, but by demographic or occupational subgroup. Two of the largest and best known are the Older Women's League and the National Association of Retired Federal Employees. Still others are membership organizations not just for older people themselves, but for professionals and academics involved in aging policy and research, such as the National Council on the Aging and the Gerontological Society of America, and the minority-based groups such as the National Caucus and Center on Black Aged and the Asociación Nacional pro Personas Mayores.

Finally, what of the disadvantaged elderly groups who are generally difficult to organize, and disinclined or unable to join organizations, such as the poor, the unemployed or lower-class nonunionized workers? It is the aging poor, as we saw in chapter 4, who are most in favor of increased government spending on the elderly. Most of the elderly organizations have attempted to diversify their demographic appeal; this has been facilitated somewhat by the use of mass mailings and media, although none of the groups has seen an influx of poor people and minorities. Advocacy for benefits targeted at the disadvantaged is often the work not of mass membership organizations, but of staff organizations funded by private philanthropies or public agencies. The Villers Foundation, staffed by professional lobbyists and policy analysts, has a distinctly low-income focus. Villers "seeks to nurture a movement of empowerment among elders," according to its brochure, placing "particular emphasis on the aged poor and near-poor," who it feels have been largely neglected by the mass membership groups.

Are any of these groups "truly" representative of the elderly? Narrowly focused groups are more likely to enjoy preference homogeneity, unity of purpose, and intensity of feeling among their members, but their limited scope decreases their credibility as representatives of the entire older population. The more broadly focused groups, on the other hand, often must adopt less controversial and less sweeping policies in order not to offend any segment of their constituency (Light 1985: 76). Some interviewees, for example, insisted that representation of a membership as diverse as AARP's is not possible; "they might as well drop the 'Retired' and call themselves the American Association of Persons," one remarked. Clearly, both narrowly and broadly focused groups have certain representational advantages.

It is more fruitful, however, to study the representativeness of interest groups collectively rather than individually. Collectively, the aging-based organizations cover a lot of ground. "Intramovement differences are often perceived . . . as conflicting," Freeman has observed of the women's movement (1975: 51), "but it is their essential complementarity that has been one of the strengths of the movement." The same could be said of the politics of aging. There may be membership overlap, and competition for members and influence among the elderly organizations, but the various representative foci complement each other as well. Aging-based organization leaders do respect each others' "turf" and the advantages of "competition of ideas" and "diversity of attack," as one leader put it. Intergroup competition for constituency loyalty can promote active participation, as groups feel compelled by market-like forces to offer greater opportunities and incentives (Hayes 1986: 143). Organizational diversity can also increase political effectiveness, as each group fights for particular parts of the elderly program (Peirce and Choharis 1982: 1562). Thus the two dilemmas— whether to support universal or means-tested benefits, and whether to portray the elderly as disadvantaged or as vital to society—turn out to be assets for the aging-based organizations.

Representative Style

The style of representation, we noted earlier, depends on the extent of rank and file participation in organizational decision making, which in turn depends on both the opportunities and the willingness of members to participate. The decision making structures of the aging-based organizations range from centralized staffs to decentralized networks of semi-autonomous local groups. The structure and representative style of each organization reflect that group's chosen balance between hierarchy and participation, in the effort to achieve both internal democracy and external effectiveness.

Is there an equilibrium between hierarchy and participation, at which both are maximized without detracting from each other? Such an equilibrium may exist in theory, but what of organizational behavior in the real world? If the behavior of the mass membership elderly organizations is any indication, there is indeed a tendency to move toward a hierarchy-participation equilibrium. This is not to say that they will all end up at the same place, but rather that organizations starting out as flat and decentralized will move toward hierarchy, while organizations starting out as highly centralized will move toward the development of decentralized subunits.

The American Association of Retired Persons is one organization that started with a centralized national structure and greatly expanded its network of local chapters and political activists nationwide. AARP has over 3,700 chapters, along with over 2,500 separate Retired Teachers Association units, and in recent years has poured more resources into developing state-level and chapter-level political work. Only about 7 percent of its members belong to local chapters, however, and AARP has also increased its political mass mailings to members. These include calls for voluntary action through committee work, petitions and letters to Congress, questionnaires on issues of importance to members, and, in the last few years, voter education materials with information about candidates and appeals for voter registration. AARP also has a large staff in Washington and a volunteer network of regional and state coordinators.

The National Committee to Preserve Social Security and Medicare and the National Alliance of Senior Citizens remain centralized in their decision making and operations, subsisting solely on membership dues and contributions gained from mass mailings and media appeals. Both have memberships largely of the "checkbook" variety, although both now survey their members on issue and position preferences, and NASC has chartered a few state chapters.

The Gray Panthers started at the other end of the centralization scale, emphasizing the autonomy and local activist focus of its chapters, or "networks." Local networks remain largely autonomous and involved in community work, and the national leadership remains committed to membership participation in decisions, through network communications, conventions, and rotating terms on the national steering committee. However, the organization has also, in recent years, developed a more hierarchical and centralized decision making structure, to increase efficiency and coordination.

The National Council of Senior Citizens has taken a number of structural turns in its history. Beginning as a specialized staff committee around the Medicare issue, it expanded to a large network of semi-autonomous state and local clubs through its ties to labor unions and the Democratic National Committee. While the emphasis remains on recruitment and participation through local and state affiliates, NCSC has begun, in the last few years, to expand its use of targeted mass mailings in order to recruit new members and coordinate activities from the national office.

Representative Types

The involvement of older Americans in the decisions and political activities of their interest groups has varied across organizations and across time. Group leaders have acted as agents, as trustees, and as stylistic hybrids combining the two. The aging-based interest groups are as diverse in style as they are in focus. Figure 1 is a sketch of the representative "landscape," with organizations placed roughly along two continuous dimensions, focus and style.[2] The placement of the groups is approximate, not quantified; it is also time-bound, since organizational focus and style may change over time. But the figure helps to compare each organization, as it operated in the mid-1980s, with the four "ideal types" in the corners of the table.

Pure membership groups, in the upper left corner, focus on the

Figure 1. Representative Focus and Style in Aging-Based Interest Groups, 1987

FOCUS

	Mass Membership	Targeted Mass Membership	Staff
Agent	"Pure Membership Groups"		"Subsidized Solidary Groups"
		Gray Panthers	
		National Association of Retired Federal Employees	
		Older Women's League	
			National Council on the Aging
STYLE	National Council of Senior Citizens		
	American Association of Retired Persons		National Caucus and Center on Black Aged
			Asociación Nacional pro Personas Mayores
	National Committee to Preserve Social Security and Medicare		
		National Alliance of Senior Citizens	Villers Foundation
Trustee	"Mass Groups"		"Pure Staff Groups"

Sources: Adapted from Eulau (1962) and Hayes (1986). The dimensions of focus and style are from Eulau; the names for the four types of groups (in quotes) are from Hayes.

[2] The figure is similar to a table proposed by Michael Hayes (1986: 137); however, Hayes's dimensions are "primary source of financial support" and "opportunity for face-to-face relations."

broadest constituency possible, use a variety of incentives to attract members, and provide maximum opportunities for member input in decision making and political support. Mass groups, in the lower corner, also focus on a broad constituency, but decisions are centralized, and member participation is mostly passive and reactive to leadership appeals. Subsidized solidary groups, in the upper right corner, are principally organizations of organizations; they have local chapters with some autonomy and access to the national leadership, but they subsist mostly on private or government grants, rather than on support from individual members. Finally, pure staff groups, in the lower right corner, operate from a single centralized office and receive financial support from grants, not from member dues or contributions.

How "representative" of older people do their mass membership organizations appear to the staff of federal agencies and on Capitol Hill? The groups' visibility and effectiveness were acclaimed widely, as we saw in chapter 5. Most interviewees also agreed that the groups' activities reflect the views of their constituents, with some qualifications. First, many recognized the "trustee" style of representation, as opposed to simple congruence between group positions and public opinion polls:

The leadership does a good job of representing the key priorities . . . doing what they have to do to preserve aging benefits and programs . . . even though the average older person would probably be more willing to sacrifice cost-of-living increases for the benefit of younger taxpayers.

They're generally more progressive, more liberal, than their members, because their members tend to join for the benefits, while the leaders are more activist. . . . But the leaders and staff have the expertise to present solutions and get things done for older people.

They do represent older people's views on Social Security and Medicare. Not many people even know anything about most of the other issues the groups push for.

Second, many took note of the decidedly middle-class bias in membership and policy positions:

Older people themselves are becoming more aware and politicized. . . . They're speaking out instead of being spoken for. . . . They're making sure the groups don't push for means-testing, even backdoor means-testing.

There's very little lobbying for low-income programs like low-income housing, Medicaid, and SSI . . . probably because they don't have low-income members.

There's almost no interest in low-income stuff, except from Villers.

Third, perceptions of leaders' representation of constituency views were highly partisan. All those who insisted that the mass membership organizations do *not* represent older people's views were Republican administration appointees, in Washington and in Sacramento:

The groups don't speak for the average elderly. Most of them are concerned about their grandchildren . . . but the interest groups ignore this. They protect themselves first, and the elderly second.

Grassroots work is important . . . [b]ut most of the groups are too partisan. They lose out when the vast majority supports the other party.

All these groups have their own agenda, but their membership comprises a small percentage of the elderly. . . . The professional organizations do a lot better in promoting senior interests than the membership organizations do.

Finally, returning to the question of leader-follower separation as reflected in public opinion polls, most older people do express satisfaction with the current level of government spending on the elderly. Although most do not advocate increases in spending on the elderly—and are even less likely to favor increases than younger adults—almost no one of any age favors *less* spending on Social Security, Medicare, and the elderly in general. Although the aging-based organizations may not be fighting an intergenerational war at the mass level, they do work, at the elite level, to protect programs and benefits that many older people favor and, perhaps, take for granted.

INTEREST GROUP REPRESENTATION IN THE POLITY AS A WHOLE

Representation by interest groups takes many forms. A large and active membership is not required; heterogeneity, unity, and cohesiveness are not required. It would seem that older people are well represented in Washington; there are effective and well-connected political organizations, mass membership organizations, staff groups representing those who are difficult to mobilize, and professional organizations supporting elderly programs and benefits. Yet, having taken the complexity of representation into account, there remains some uneasiness in the literature about the representativeness of aging-based interest groups. The uneasiness comes not from considering the organizations individually or even collectively, but from viewing their role in the political process as a whole. Two major perspectives guide the critique of interest group representation: interest group liberalism, and political economy. Both perspectives share the conclusion that "more interest groups" does not mean "more representation."

The interest group liberalism view argues that, whatever the contours of interest group activity, the American political system favors narrow interests over broad publics.[3] Interest groups may achieve visibility and legitimacy within the system, succeeding in political battles for incremental changes without achieving economic redistribution or social justice on a broader scale. The aging-based interest groups, to illustrate, enjoy a great deal of legitimacy and influence; elites circulate among government staff positions and interest group staff positions, maintaining personal ties between organizations and policy makers. Still, poverty or near-poverty continue to plague a large percentage of the elderly. Binstock (1972: 278), applying this perspective to aging politics, concludes that

> the case of the aged suggests that a group can attain political equality—as measured by . . . political scientists . . . without achieving social and economic justice. To focus on "representation" by elected officials and "representation" through the bargaining of organized groups in assessing the citizen's means of access to power is to set aside ultimate issues of social justice, and to ignore what may be more important avenues to power.

The political economy perspective, focusing on inequalities and injustices inherent in capitalist market economies, sees the elderly as a group that is isolated and subjugated, rather than helped, by aging policies. The "aging enterprise," as Estes has labeled it—the "programs, organizations, bureaucracies, interest groups, trade associations, providers, industries, and professionals that serve the aged," actually stigmatize older people, treat them as a "problem," remove them from the labor force, and attempt to isolate them from broader political movements (Estes 1979: 2). Aging policies perpetuate the class structures or inequalities that exist prior to old age, rather than helping to alleviate them. Aging policy is, in fact, not meant to deal with the problems of older people, but rather to control and coopt the interests of exploited

---

[3] See, in particular, Lowi (1979); McConnell (1966); and Schattschneider (1960).

groups and, in particular, to control the labor market (Estes 1979, 1984; Hudson and Strate 1985: 578–80; Nelson 1982; Olson 1982).

Both perspectives view the representation of narrow interests as incomplete or irrelevant at best, anathema at worst, to the representation of the disadvantaged classes or of the society as a whole. What is the remedy? The organization of interests must be supplanted, or at least supplemented, by broader coalitions that transcend narrow concerns. Some look to strengthened party organizations as best able to mobilize broad interests—especially those of the poor and disadvantaged—and to set the agenda for economic justice and redistribution (Berry 1984: 219; Cigler and Loomis 1986: 305; Schlozman and Tierney 1986: 403). Others, noting the lack of a Socialist or Labor party alternative in the United States, look instead to "a new, forceful coalition"—not a "coalition of the poor aged and the wealthy aged," but one that "would consist of severely disadvantaged persons from within each of many traditionally defined groups" (Binstock 1972: 279; see also Estes 1979: 230).

Is this possible in the United States? There is some precedent to suggest the possibility. Most sweeping changes in aging policy have been the result of coalition work—for example, the fight for Medicare alongside organized labor and other interest groups (Williamson et al. 1982). Generations United, a coalition of advocacy groups rejecting the charge that domestic social welfare programs are zero-sum, with some needy groups gaining only at the expense of others, is the latest such attempt. Such coalitions, however, tend to be temporary, not highly visible, and confined to one or a few specific issues (Berry 1984: 202–5). Their enduring success, outside of partisan politics, remains to be seen.

CHAPTER 7

Conclusion

THE organizational and political success of old-age interest groups has expanded dramatically since midcentury. These organizations now possess a wealth of political resources, including mass memberships, healthy finances, well-known lobbyists, and easy access to many government officials. The elderly's financial situation, furthermore, has improved markedly; poverty is lower, net worth is higher, medical care is more accessible, and all of these gains have been faster for older people than for the rest of the population.

The progress enjoyed by older Americans as a group, and by the organizations representing them, has made them targets for critics who charge that the elderly have received more than their fair share from government. The critics—in politics, journalism, and academia—portray the elderly as a relatively affluent group backed by a powerful and greedy lobby.

The censure of old-age political organizations reflects popular contemporary criticism of interest groups in general. Interest groups, their detractors say, inhibit the efforts of elected officials to govern in the public interest; fail to represent accurately their constituencies' opinions; restrict policies to minor alterations rather than broad, sweeping changes; and constrain the parties' efforts to build broad coalitions. These judgments, like most stereotypes, contain a grain of truth but are misleading in their simplicity. This study of the politics of aging helps to illuminate the fact and the fallacy behind each of these four charges against modern interest groups.

INTEREST GROUPS AND THE PUBLIC INTEREST

Do interest groups, with their narrow, selfish demands, inhibit the efforts of elected officials to govern in the public interest? The growth of elderly influence and well-being has indeed generated charges of selfishness and special privilege. The accusations come from within government and from without: complaints that old-age pressures prevent policy makers from cutting the budget sufficiently to reduce the deficit. Government, they say, feels compelled to use its limited resources for pleasing the elderly lobby, rather than for other purposes, ranging from education and pollution to foreign aid and national defense.

Yet many elected officials are aided, not inhibited, by old-age interest groups. The organizations conduct research, collect information, and provide public and financial support helpful to policy makers. Advocates of old-age benefits in the national and state legislatures use the interest groups' information and endorsements to help advance their own legislative priorities. Agency officials involved with aging policy at all levels of government cultivate alliances with the interest groups, to demonstrate that their programs enjoy public support. Government does not simply react to interest group pressures; in many cases government supports and encourages them.

Nor do these alliances between groups and government necessarily result in narrow policies being forced upon an unwilling public. Older people are not the only beneficiaries of old-age policy gains. Younger people will profit when they, too, reach old age; they benefit currently as well in bearing less responsibility for their aging relatives. The elderly, furthermore, are a highly legitimate recipient group; surveys show that support for old-age government benefits is high across all age groups of adults, as we saw in chapter 3.

There may be some merit to the argument that today's older generation is draining the resources from future generations of older people, particularly if Social Security and Medicare face the danger of bankruptcy, as some analysts have predicted. Still, the high degree of public support for old-age programs and benefits contradicts the notion of a selfish interest opposing "the people" and their elected officials.

CONSTITUENCY REPRESENTATION

Do interest groups fail to represent accurately their constituencies' opinions? Comparing the positions taken by old-age organizations with the aging policy opinions analyzed in chapter three may lead to the conclusion that there is indeed a gap between leaders and followers. While most of the old-age organizations pressure government for increases in government spending on the elderly, the elderly themselves do not overwhelmingly support those increases. Younger adults, in fact, tend to support those increases more than older people. Members of the aging-based interest groups, furthermore, do not necessarily join because they back the organizations' political positions. These organizations attract some members by offering other incentives—goods and services, friends and social outlets, for example—that have little to do with political attitudes. Group leaders, once their group is established, take control of organizational decision making—the effect that Michels described as the "iron law of oligarchy." The leaders then claim to speak for their members, whether members have joined for political reasons or for other motives.

Another look at the public opinion survey data, however, indicates that these groups' political activities are not so contrary to elderly opinion after all. Older people, in the first place, are sharply divided on aging policy issues, with those in greatest need showing the most support for spending increases on the elderly. From the perspective of the most needy, the organizational issue positions are not only not excessively radical; they often do not go far enough.

Second, the vast majority of older people are not against government benefits for the elderly; they simply are satisfied with what they have. Almost no one says spending on the elderly should be decreased; they say it is "about right" at the current level. If few older people list aging policy as one of their top political priorities, it may be because they take for granted the very benefits that the elderly organizations are fighting to maintain.

Finally, the history of aging politics shows that elderly interest groups were not simply created by entrepreneurs and "sold" to a potential constituency. The elderly political movement arose, early in the twentieth century, out of social changes that created new hardships and objective needs for many older Americans. Government policies to alleviate these needs led to rising expectations of public responsibility, which led to broader support for old-age benefits and more political activity on behalf of older people. Today's aging-based interest group leaders have used a variety of resources and incentives to build and maintain their organizations, but they did not begin in a political vacuum. The foundation for old-age political activity was laid decades ago.

INTEREST GROUPS AND POLITICAL CHANGE

Do interest groups restrict policies to minor alterations rather than broad, sweeping changes? This is a difficult question to answer, but not because there is a false distinction between distributive and redistributive policy, or between incremental and nonincremental change. The distinction is valid, if imprecise. What is difficult is speculating on what might have been. If the contours of group involvement had been different, in other words, would the resulting policy have been more redistributive? More incremental?

The aging-based organizations have been advocates of a variety of

policies, some minor, some far-reaching. As a fledgling social movement before Social Security was enacted, elderly political activity re-
volved around major, redistributive, but politically implausible solutions such as the Townsend Plan. The political effects of such activity
are still in dispute; some assert it was too far out of the mainstream,
while others claim that it helped put aging issues onto the political
agenda. During the 1950s through the early 1970s, when most present-day elderly organizations were becoming established and struggling to maintain themselves, most of their solo activity focused upon
distributive policies such as small programs funded under the Older
Americans Act; more impressive elderly gains were achieved with the
help of established allies such as organized labor.

Now that the aging-based organizations have matured and institutionalized, their politics has become at once more pragmatic and more
daring. They have learned to use "insider" lobbying strategies, to compromise and to offer practical solutions. At the same time, they are
pressing for such sweeping programs as more comprehensive medical
insurance and long-term care, at a time when the federal deficit is cre-
ating pressures to cut back on social spending. This evolutionary pattern, from "fringe" social movement to institutionalized interest
group, is common among broad constituencies such as older people,
women, minorities, evangelists, tax revolters, and many others at all
points on the political spectrum. The achievement of insider status
does not necessarily imply adherence to the status quo.

INTEREST GROUPS AND POLITICAL PARTIES

Do interest groups inhibit the parties' efforts to build broad coalitions? Political parties must appeal to as wide a spectrum of the population as possible, and over the long term, in order to elect candidates
and govern effectively. Their appeal, therefore, is based on broad principles, common goals, and coherent policy programs. The parochial
and uncompromising demands of interest groups, so goes the argument, tend to pull apart the coalitions that parties have put together.
The parties may find themselves making concessions to interests rather
than compromises among them, resulting in fragmented, redundant,
or contradictory platforms and policies.

This is often true, but not always. Sometimes, interest groups actually help, rather than hinder, the coalition-building process, providing
important mass support for certain partisan issue positions already in
place. The National Council of Senior Citizens (NCSC) is the purest
example, among aging-based interest groups, of a party-interest group

alliance. NCSC, an offshoot of organized labor, was created out of the Senior Citizens for Kennedy and the pro-Medicare efforts of the Democratic party.

Most of the other aging-based organizations, in contrast, have remained self-consciously bipartisan, attempting to inject old-age issues into the politics of both parties, and avoiding outright partisan endorsements. Their constituency is quite evenly divided along party lines, and their needs are diverse; therefore it makes political sense for the organizations to maintain a bipartisan posture. The same could be said about many interest groups in this country, elderly and nonelderly alike.

The diverse experiences of old-age political organizations suggest that some interest groups do indeed inhibit the parties' coalition-building efforts, while others facilitate those efforts. Does it make any difference to the constituency? The elderly as a group have benefited from many government policies over the past several decades, and aging-based organizations can be credited for influencing some of those beneficial policies, particularly during the past decade or two. The economic progress enjoyed by the elderly, however, has been uneven; the gap between rich and poor older people has widened as older people have seen their collective fortunes improve. Inequalities among older Americans persist, despite the achievements of old-age interest groups. Millions of older people remain in poverty; many millions more are near enough to the poverty line to be struggling financially. Older Americans' attitudes toward aging policy, furthermore, divide along economic and partisan lines, rather than manifesting old-age interest group unity.

Critics of interest groups charge that groups alone are rarely able to develop and influence broad, coherent, redistributive policies; this is more the province of political parties. This has been a popular theme in political science for over a century. Tocqueville, early in the nineteenth century, recognized the integrative function of parties: "In the absence of great parties, the United States swarm with lesser controversies; and public opinion is divided into a thousand minute shades of difference upon questions of detail" (1945: pt. 1, chap. 8). Schattschneider, in 1960, called for strong, responsible political parties to correct the upper-class bias of interest groups.

Many scholars in the past decade have echoed these ideas, calling for stronger, principled, and disciplined parties. The political parties are capable of aggregating narrow interests into broad economic and social concerns, replacing a piecemeal and contradictory set of policies with a coherent political agenda. Party programs, furthermore, include proposals designed to meet the needs of unorganized, as well as organized, constituencies. A stronger, centralized party system therefore provides an antidote to an unpredictable and ungovernable system of competitive groups. Party defenders argue, furthermore, that many interest groups have emerged to fill the gap left by weakened party organizations, and that if the parties were stronger, interest groups would be neither as numerous nor as powerful as they are today.

INTEREST GROUPS, POLITICAL PARTIES, AND AMERICAN POLITICS

Political parties may indeed provide some coherence and continuity to the political system more easily than interest groups. Strong political parties, however, are not in themselves the panacea for the fragmentation and the biases of American politics, particularly if the parties systematically exclude certain interests. Party organizations prefer to elect leaders and govern with the minimum possible amount of internal conflict. Their best strategy for minimizing internal conflict is to integrate the smallest number of diverse groups that would still be sufficient to assure electoral victory.

Interest groups can work with political parties to prevent certain sectors of society from being left out of partisan politics and party platforms. Interest groups do not necessarily drive parties out of business. They may in fact complement, enhance, and broaden the scope of the parties, forcing the parties to integrate new constituencies and new issues into the agenda. Abolitionists, integrationists, feminists, conservationists, evangelists—and supporters of such "socialistic" programs as Social Security and Medicare—are all examples of "extremist" groups that have moved, or are moving, into the American political mainstream, and often into partisan alliances.

Political parties are not the only organizations capable of forming alliances. Extra-partisan coalitions of interest groups are increasingly prevalent. The aging-based organizations have played a leading role in at least two intergenerational coalitions during the past decade. One is Save Our Security, which united successfully to fight President Reagan's proposed Social Security cuts in the early 1980s. The other coalition is Generations United, formed in reaction to critics who charge that excessive old-age benefits deplete government resources for today's children and for future generations of older people.

Interest group coalitions, however, tend to arise primarily in reaction to perceived threats, are often limited to a single issue, and are usually temporary and less inclusive than political parties. Cooperation between parties and interest groups—including the creation of new parties if the established ones fail to accommodate certain interests—is the best strategy for achieving both ideological consistency and comprehensive representation in American politics.

Survey Questions and Coding of Variables

Spending on the Elderly

How about the U.S. government? Given all the expenses the government has, would you say it is spending as much as it should on the elderly, more that it should or not as much as it should?
[Coding for probit analysis: 0 = as much as it should or more than it should; 1 = not as much as it should.]

Medicare Cutbacks

Which of the following statements comes closer to your own view? (A) Under no circumstances should Medicare aid to the elderly be cut back. (B) Because of the financial crunch, Medicare, like other government programs, should be cut back.

Mandatory Retirement

Would you favor or oppose having a mandatory retirement age, after which employers no longer permit workers to stay on the job full-time?

Personal Problems

I'm going to read you some problems that people have mentioned to us. For each, will you please tell me how much of a problem it is for you personally: a very serious problem, a serious problem, a minor problem or no problem at all: not enough medical care; not having enough money to live on. [Coding for probit analysis: 1 = no problem; 2 = minor problem; 3 = serious problem; 4 = very serious problem.]

National Economy

Do you think the nation's economy is getting better, getting worse or staying the same? [Coding for probit analysis: 1 = getting better; 2 = staying the same; 3 = getting worse.]

Personal Finances

Looking ahead, do you think that a year from now you personally will be better off financially, worse off or in about the same state as now? [Coding for probit analysis: 1 = better off; 2 = same as now; 3 = worse off.]

Sources of Income

Can you tell me whether anyone in your household receives Social Security for the elderly from the federal government?
Would you say that more than half or less than half of your total household income comes from Social Security payments? [Coding for probit analysis: 0 = none or less than half; 1 = more than half.]

Aside from Social Security, are you yourself covered by any kind of pension or profit-sharing plan? Is anyone else in the household covered?

Does anyone in your household get Medicare assistance, that is, government help in paying medical bills for older people?
And does anyone in your household get Medicaid assistance, that is, government help in paying medical bills for those who couldn't pay otherwise?

AMERICAN NATIONAL ELECTION STUDIES

Federal Spending

If you had a say in making up the federal budget this year, which programs would you like to see increased and which reduced: protecting and improving the environment; dealing with crime; public schools; Social Security; Food Stamps; Medicare; government jobs for the unemployed; science and technology; defense; assistance to blacks? (1984)

Medical Insurance

There is much concern about the rapid rise in medical and hospital costs. Some feel there should be a government insurance plan which would cover all medical and hospital expenses. Others feel that medical expenses should be paid by individuals, and through private insurance like Blue Cross. Where would you place yourself on this scale, or haven't you thought much about this? [7-point scale] (1976, 1978)

There is much concern about the rapid rise in medical and hospital costs. Some feel there should be a government insurance plan which would cover all medical and hospital expenses for everyone. Others feel that medical expenses should be paid by individuals, and through private insurance like Blue Cross. Where would you place yourself on this scale, or haven't you thought much about this? [7-point scale] (1984)

Most Important National Problem

What do you think are the most important problems facing this country? (Anything else?) [up to three responses]

Group Identification

Here is a list of groups. Please read over the list and tell me the letter for those groups you feel particularly close to—people who are most like you in their ideas and interests and feelings about things. . . . Look at the list again. Of the groups you mentioned, which one do you feel closest to?
Sometimes people think about other groups of people in society when they think about their own economic well-being, people who are being helped or hurt by economic conditions. When it comes to economic matters, what groups of people do you feel close to? (If respondent doesn't know what we mean by "groups"): Some people have mentioned farmers, the elderly, teachers, blacks, and union members. . . . When it comes to economic matters, what sorts of people do you feel closest to?

Personal Finances

We are interested in how people are getting along financially these days. Would you say that you (and your family living here) are better off or worse off financially than you were a year ago?

Elderly Economic Position

What about the elderly? Would you say that over the past year the economic position of the elderly has gotten better, stayed about the same, or gotten worse?

National Economy

How about the economy? Would you say that over the past year the nation's economy has gotten better, stayed the same or gotten worse?

NORC GENERAL SOCIAL SURVEY

Federal Spending

We are faced with many problems in this country, none of which can be solved easily or inexpensively. I'm going to name some of these problems, and for each one I'd like you to tell me whether you think we're spending too much money on it, too little money, or about the right amount: space exploration program; improving and protecting the environment; improving and protecting the nation's health; solving the problems of the big cities; halting the rising crime rate; dealing with drug addiction; improving the nation's education system; improving the conditions of blacks; the military, armaments and defense; foreign aid; welfare; [added in 1984] highways and bridges; Social Security; mass transportation; parks and recreation.

DEMOGRAPHIC AND SOCIOECONOMIC
VARIABLES: ALL SURVEYS

Income was coded into two categories: above and below the median income for the sample. Coding for probit analysis: 1 = under $8,000; 2 = $8,000 but less than $12,000; 3 = $12,000 but less than $20,000; 4 = $20,000 but less than $30,000; 5 = $30,000 but less than $50,000; 6 = $50,000 or more.

Education was coded into three categories: less than high school graduate; high school graduate; and some college or more. Coding for probit analysis: 1 = eighth grade or less; 2 = some high school; 3 = graduated high school; 4 = some college; 5 = graduated college; 6 = postgraduate.

Subjective social class was divided into the two major categories: working class and middle class. Coding for probit analysis: 0 = working class; 1 = middle class.

Political party was coded into three categories: Democrat, Republican, and Independent. Respondents who leaned toward one party or another were coded into those parties, not as Independents. Coding for probit analysis: 1 = strong Democrat; 2 = Democrat; 3 = weak Democrat; 4 = Independent; 5 = weak Republican; 6 = Republican; 7 = strong Republican.

Ideology was collapsed into three categories: liberal, moderate, and conservative. Coding for probit analysis: 1 = very liberal; 2 = somewhat liberal; 3 = moderate; 4 = somewhat conservative; 5 = very conservative.

Retirement status Coding for probit analysis: 0 = not retired; 1 = retired.

Race Coding for probit analysis: 0 = white; 1 = black or Hispanic.

Sex Coding for probit analysis: 0 = male; 1 = female.

Marital status Coding for probit analysis: 0 = married; 1 = separated, divorced, widowed, or never married.

Age For probit analysis, age is a continuous variable.

ABC News and *The Washington Post*. 1982. *ABC News/Washington Post Poll of Public Opinion on Aging, March 1982*. Machine-readable data file. New York and Washington, D.C.: ABC News and *The Washington Post*.

Achenbaum, W. Andrew. 1978. *Old Age in the New Land: The American Experience Since 1790*. Baltimore: Johns Hopkins University Press.

———. 1986. *Social Security: Visions and Revisions*. Cambridge: Cambridge University Press.

Aldrich, John H., and Charles F. Cnudde. 1975. "Probing the Bounds of Conventional Wisdom: A Comparison of Regression, Probit, and Discriminant Analysis." *American Journal of Political Science* 19: 571–608.

Aldrich, John H., and Forrest D. Nelson. 1984. *Linear Probability, Logit, and Probit Models*. Beverly Hills: Sage.

American Demographics. 1984. "Demographic Forecasts: Elderly Incomes." *American Demographics* 6 (November): 50.

Babchuck, Nicholas, George R. Peters, Danny R. Hoyt, and Marvin A. Kaiser. 1979. "The Voluntary Associations of the Aged." *Journal of Gerontology* 34: 579–87.

Bachrach, Peter. 1967. *The Theory of Democratic Elitism: A Critique*. Boston: Little, Brown.

Bachrach, Peter, and Morton S. Baratz. 1962. "Two Faces of Power." *American Political Science Review* 56: 947–52.

Beauvoir, Simone de. 1972. *The Coming of Age*. New York: Putnam's.

Bengtson, Vern L., Neal E. Cutler, David J. Mangen, and Victor W. Marshall. 1985. In Robert H. Binstock and Ethel Shanas, eds., *Handbook of Aging and the Social Sciences*, 2d ed. New York: Van Nostrand Reinhold.

Bentley, Arthur F. 1908. *The Process of Government*. Chicago: University of Chicago Press.

Berger, Suzanne. 1981. *Organizing Interests in Western Europe*. Cambridge: Cambridge University Press.

Berry, Jeffrey M. 1977. *Lobbying for the People*. Princeton: Princeton University Press.

———. 1984. *The Interest Group Society*. Boston: Little, Brown.

Binstock, Robert H. 1972. "Interest-Group Liberalism and the Politics of Aging." *Gerontologist* 12: 265–80.

———. 1981. "The Politics of Aging Interest Groups: Interest Group Liberalism and the Politics of Aging." In Robert B. Hudson, ed., *The Aging in Politics*. Springfield, Ill.: Charles C. Thomas.

———. 1983. "The Aged as Scapegoat." *Gerontologist* 23: 136–43.

Binstock, Robert H., Martin A. Levin, and Richard Weatherly. 1985. "Political Dilemmas of Social Intervention." In Robert H. Binstock and Ethel

Shanas, eds., *Handbook of Aging and the Social Sciences*, 2d ed. New York: Van Nostrand Reinhold.

Brody, Richard A., and Paul M. Sniderman. 1977. "From Life Space to Polling Place.: The Relevance of Personal Concerns for Voting Behavior." *British Journal of Political Science* 7: 337–60.

Brown, E. Richard. 1984. "Medicare and Medicaid: The Process, Value and Limits of Health Care Reforms." In Meredith Minkler and Carroll L. Estes, eds., *Readings in the Political Economy of Aging*. Farmingdale, N.Y.: Baywood.

Browne, William P., and Laura Katz Olson, eds. 1983. *Aging and Public Policy: The Politics of Growing Old in America*. Westport, Conn.: Greenwood Press.

Campbell, Angus. 1971. "Politics Through the Life Cycle." *Gerontologist* 11: 112–17.

Campbell, Angus, Philip E. Converse, Warren E. Miller, and Donald E. Stokes. 1960. *The American Voter*. New York: John Wiley.

Campbell, John Creighton, and John Strate. 1981. "Are Old People Conservative?" *Gerontologist* 21: 580–91.

Carlie, Michael Kaye. 1969. "The Politics of Age: Interest Group or Social Movement?" *Gerontologist* 9: 259–64.

Chong, Dennis. 1987. "Public-Spirited Collective Action." Paper presented at the Annual Meeting of the American Political Science Association, Chicago, Illinois.

Cigler, Allan J., and John Mark Hansen. 1983. "Group Formation through Protest: The American Agriculture Movement." In Allan J. Cigler and Burdett A. Loomis, ed., *Interest Group Politics*. Washington, D.C.: Congressional Quarterly Press.

Cigler, Allan J., and Burdett A. Loomis. 1983. "Introduction: The Changing Nature of Interest Group Politics." In Allan J. Cigler and Burdett A. Loomis, eds., *Interest Group Politics*. Washington, D.C.: Congressional Quarterly Press.

———. 1986. "Moving On: Interests, Power, and Politics in the 1980s." In Allan J. Cigler and Burdett A. Loomis, eds., *Interest Group Politics*, 2d ed. Washington, D.C.: Congressional Quarterly Press.

Clark, Peter B., and James Q. Wilson. 1961. "Incentive Systems: A Theory of Organizations." *Administrative Science Quarterly* 6: 219–66.

Clemente, Frank. 1975. "Age and the Perception of National Priorities." *Gerontologist* 15: 61–63.

Conover, Pamela Johnston. 1984. "The Influence of Group Identifications on Political Percpetions and Evaluations." *Journal of Politics* 46: 760–85.

———. 1985. "Studying Group Influence: What Do the Measures Mean?" Paper presented at the Annual Meeting of the American Political Science Association, New Orleans, Louisiana.

Converse, Philip E. 1964. "The Nature of Belief Systems in Mass Publics." In David E. Apter, ed., *Ideology and Discontent*. New York: Free Press.

Conway, M. Margaret. 1985. *Political Participation in the United States*. Washington, D.C.: Congressional Quarterly Press.

Cook, Constance Ewing. 1984. "Participation in Public Interest Groups: Membership Motivations." *American Politics Quarterly* 12: 409–30.

Costain, Anne N., and W. Douglas Costain. 1983. "The Women's Lobby: Impact of a Movement on Congress." In Allan J. Cigler and Burdett A. Loomis, eds., *Interest Group Politics*. Washington, D.C.: Congressional Quarterly Press.

Cutler, Neal E. 1977. "Demographic, Social-Psychological, and Political Factors in the Politics of Aging: A Foundation for Research in 'Political Gerontology.' " *American Political Science Review* 71: 1011–25.

———. 1981. "Political Characteristics of Elderly Cohorts in the Twenty-First Century." In Sara B. Keisler, James N. Morgan and Valerie Kincaid Oppenheimer, eds., *Aging: Social Change*. New York: Academic Press.

———. 1984. "Federal and State Responsibilities and the Targeting of Resources within the Older Americans Act: The Dynamics of Multiple Agenda-Setting." *Policy Studies Journal* 12: 185–96.

Cutler, Neal E., and Vern L. Bengtson. 1974. "Age and Political Alienation: Maturation, Generation and Period Effects." *Annals of the American Academy of Political and Social Science* 415: 160–75.

Cutler, Neal E., and John R. Schmidhauser. 1975. "Age and Political Behavior." In Diane S. Woodruff and James E. Birren, eds., *Scientific Perspectives and Social Issues*. New York: D. Van Nostrand.

Cutler, Stephen J. 1977. "Aging and Voluntary Association Participation." *Journal of Gerontology* 32: 470–79.

Dahl, Robert A. 1956. *A Preface to Democratic Theory*. Chicago: University of Chicago Press.

———. 1961. *Who Governs?* New Haven: Yale University Press.

Davis, James A., and Tom W. Smith. 1984. *General Social Survey Cumulative File, 1972–1984*. Machine-readable data file. National Opinion Research Center. Chicago: University of Chicago.

De Grazia, Alfred. 1951. *Public and Republic: Political Representation in America*. New York: Alfred A. Knopf.

Demkovich, Linda E. 1984. "The Golden Years." *National Journal* (October 20): 1992.

Derthick, Martha. 1979a. "How Easy Votes on Social Security Came to an End." *The Public Interest* 54: 94–105.

———. 1979b. *Policymaking for Social Security*. Washington, D.C.: Brookings Institution.

Dobson, Douglas. 1983. "The Elderly as a Political Force." In William P. Browne and Laura Katz Olson, eds., *Aging and Public Policy: The Politics of Growing Old in America*. Westport, Conn.: Greenwood Press.

Dobson, Douglas, and Douglas St. Angelo. 1980. *Politics and Senior Citizens: Advocacy and Policy Formation in a Local Context*. Washington, D.C.: U.S. Administration on Aging.

Douglass, Elizabeth B., William P. Cleveland, and George L. Maddox. 1974. "Political Attitudes, Age, and Aging: A Cohort Analysis of Archival Data." *Journal of Gerontology* 29: 666–75.

Duncan, Greg J., Martha Hill, and Willard Rogers. 1986. "The Changing Fortunes of Young and Old." *American Demographics* 8 (August): 26–33.

Eckstein, Harry. 1975. "Case Study and Theory in Political Science." In Fred I. Greenstein and Nelson W. Polsby, eds., *Handbook of Political Science* Vol. 7, "Strategies of Inquiry." Reading, Mass.: Addison-Wesley.

Elder, Charles D., and Roger W. Cobb. 1984. "Agenda-Building and the Politics of Aging." *Policy Studies Journal* 13: 115–29.

Estes, Carroll L. 1978. "Political Gerontology." *Society* 15 (July/August): 43–49.

———. 1979. *The Aging Enterprise.* San Francisco: Jossey-Bass.

———. 1983. "Austerity and Aging in the United States: 1980 and Beyond." In Anne-Marie Guillemard, ed., *Old Age and the Welfare State.* Beverly Hills: Sage.

———. 1984. "Austerity and Aging: 1980 and Beyond." In Meredith Minkler and Carroll L. Estes, eds., *Readings in the Political Economy of Aging.* Farmingdale, N.Y.: Baywood.

Eulau, Heinz. 1962. "The Legislator as Representative: Representational Roles." In John C. Wahlke, Heinz Eulau, William Buchanan, and LeRoy C. Ferguson, eds., *The Legislative System: Explorations in Legislative Behavior.* New York: John Wiley.

Evans, Linda, and John B. Williamson. 1984. "Social Control of the Elderly." In Meredith Minkler and Carroll L. Estes, eds., *Readings in the Political Economy of Aging.* Farmingdale, N.Y.: Baywood.

Fessler, Pamela. 1984. "Tactics of New Elderly Lobby Ruffle Congressional Feathers." *Congressional Quarterly Weekly Report*, June 2: 1310–13.

Fessler, Pamela, and Harrison Donnelly. 1981. "Congress Seeking to Assure Retirement Income Security." *Congressional Quarterly Weekly Report*, November 28: 2333–36.

Fischer, David Hackett. 1979. "The Politics of Aging in America: A Short History." *Journal of the Institute for Socioeconomic Studies* 4: 51–66.

Foner, Anne, and Karen Schwab. 1983. "Work and Retirement in a Changing Society." In Matilda White Riley, Beth B. Hess, and K. Bond, eds., *Aging in Society: Selected Reviews of Recent Research.* Hillsdale, N.J.: Lawrence Erlbaum.

Fowler, Linda L., and Ronald G. Shaiko. 1987. "The Graying of the Constituency: Active Seniors in Congressional District Politics." Paper presented at the Annual Meeting of the American Political Science Association, Chicago, Illinois.

Fox, Richard G. 1981. "The Welfare State and the Political Mobilization of the Elderly." In Sara B. Keisler, James N. Morgan, and Valerie K. Oppenheimer, eds., *Aging: Social Change.* New York: Academic Press.

Franke, James L., and Douglas Dobson. 1985. "Interest Groups: The Problem of Representation." *Western Politics Quarterly* 38: 224–37.

Freeman, Jo. 1975. *The Politics of Women's Liberation*. New York: Longman.

Friedmann, Eugene A., and Donald J. Adamchak. 1983. "Societal Aging and Intergenerational Support Systems." In Anne-Marie Guillemard, ed., *Old Age and the Welfare State*. Beverly Hills: Sage.

Gais, Thomas L., Mark A. Peterson, and Jack L. Walker. 1984. "Interest Groups, Iron Triangles and Representative Institutions in American National Government." *British Journal of Political Science* 14: 161–85.

Gallup Report. 1985. "Majority Sees Deficit Threat; Priority Given to Defense Cuts." *The Gallup Report* (June): 2–7.

Garson, G. David. 1978. *Group Theories of Politics*. Beverly Hills: Sage.

Gerth, H.H., and C. Wright Mills. 1946. *From Max Weber: Essays in Sociology*. New York: Oxford University Press.

Gilbert, Neil. 1970. *Clients or Constituents: Community Action in the War on Poverty*. San Francisco: Jossey-Bass.

———. 1977. "The Burgeoning Social Service Payload." *Society* 14 (May/June): 63–65.

Graebner, William. 1980. *A History of Retirement: The Meaning and Function of An American Institution, 1885–1978*. New Haven: Yale University Press.

Greenstone, J. David, ed. 1982. *Public Values and Private Power in American Politics*. Chicago: University of Chicago Press.

Guillemard, Anne-Marie. 1983. "Introduction." In Anne-Marie Guillemard, ed., *Old Age and the Welfare State*. Beverly Hills: Sage.

Haas, Lawrence J. 1987. "Big-Ticket Restrictions." *National Journal*, September 26: 2413–18.

Hamilton, Alexander, John Jay, and James Madison. 1961. *The Federalist Papers*. New York: Mentor.

Hanna, William J. 1981. "Advocacy and the Elderly." In Richard H. Davis, ed., *Aging: Prospects and Issues*, 3d edition. Los Angeles: Ethel Percy Andrus Gerontology Center, University of Southern California.

Hansen, John Mark. 1985. "The Political Economy of Group Membership." *American Political Science Review* 79: 79–96.

Hanushek, Eric A., and John E. Jackson. 1977. *Statistical Methods for Social Scientists*. New York: Academic Press.

Hardin, Russell. 1982. *Collective Action*. Baltimore: Johns Hopkins University Press.

Harootyan, Robert A. 1981. "Interest Groups and Aging Policy: Interest Groups and the Development of Federal Legislation Affecting Older Americans." In Robert B. Hudson, ed., *The Aging in Politics*. Springfield, Ill.: Charles C. Thomas.

Hayes, Michael T. 1983. "Interest Groups: Pluralism or Mass Society?" In Allan J. Cigler and Burdett A. Loomis, eds., *Interest Group Politics*. Washington, D.C.: Congressional Quarterly Press.

Hayes, Michael T. 1986. "The New Group Universe." In Allan J. Cigler and Burdett A. Loomis, eds., *Interest Group Politics*, 2d ed. Washington, D.C.: Congressional Quarterly Press.

Herzog, A. Regula, Willard L. Rodgers, and Joseph Woodworth. 1982. *Subjective Well-Being Among Different Age Groups*. Ann Arbor: Institute for Social Research, University of Michigan.

Hess, Beth B. 1978. "The Politics of Aging." *Society* 15 (July/August): 22–23.

Heydebrand, Wolf V., ed. 1973. *Comparative Organizations: The Results of Empirical Research*. Englewood Cliffs: Prentice-Hall.

Hirschman, Albert O. 1970. *Exit, Voice, and Loyalty*. Cambridge, Mass.: Harvard University Press.

Holtzman, Abraham. 1963. *The Townsend Movement: A Political Study*. New York: Bookman Associates.

Hudson, Robert B. 1978. "Emerging Pressures on Public Policies for the Aging." *Society* 15 (July/August): 30–33.

———. 1980. "Old-Age Politics in a Period of Change." In Edgar F. Borgatta and Neil G. McCluskey, eds., *Aging and Society: Current Research and Perspectives*. Beverly Hills: Sage.

———. 1982. "Accounting for Old-Age Policy: A Review Essay." *National Forum* 62 (Fall): 33–35.

———, ed. 1981. *The Aging in Politics*. Springfield, Ill.: Charles C. Thomas.

Hudson, Robert B., and John Strate. 1985. "Aging and Political Systems." In Robert H. Binstock and Ethel Shanas, eds., *Handbook of Aging and the Social Sciences*, 2d ed. New York: Van Nostrand Reinhold.

Jackson, Jacquelyne Johnson. 1983. "The Politicization of Aged Blacks." In William P. Browne and Laura Katz Olson, eds., *Aging and Public Policy: The Politics of Growing Old in America*. Westport, Conn.: Greenwood Press.

Jacobs, Ruth H. 1980. "Portrait of a Phenomenon—The Gray Panthers: Do They Have a Long-Run Future?" In Elizabeth W. Markson and Gretchen R. Batra, eds., *Public Policies for an Aging Population*. Lexington, Mass.: Lexington Books, D.C. Heath and Co.

Jacobs, Ruth H., and Beth Hess. 1978. "Panther Power: Symbol and Substance." *Long Term Care and Health Services Administration Quarterly* 2: 238–44.

Janda, Kenneth. 1968. "Representation: Representational Behavior." In David L. Sills, ed., *International Encyclopedia of the Social Sciences*, Vol 13. N.Y.: Macmillan/Free Press.

Katz, Michael B. 1986. *In the Shadow of the Poorhouse: A Social History of Welfare in America*. New York: Basic Books.

Keith, Jennie. 1981. "Old Age and Age Differentiation: Anthropological Speculations on Age as a Social Border." In Sara B. Keisler, James N. Morgan, and Valerie Kincaid Oppenheimer, eds., *Aging: Social Change*. New York: Academic Press.

Kerschner, Paul A., ed. 1976. *Advocacy and Age.* Los Angeles: Ethel Percy Andrus Gerontology Center, University of Southern California.

Kesselman, Mark. 1982. "The Conflictual Evolution of American Political Science: From Apologetic Pluralism to Trilateralism and Marxism." In J. David Greenstone, ed., *Public Values and Private Power in American Politics.* Chicago: University of Chicago Press.

Key, V. O., Jr. 1961. *Public Opinion and American Policy.* New York: Alfred A. Knopf.

Kinder, Donald R., Gordon S. Adams, and Paul W. Gronke. 1985. "Economics and Politics in 1984." Paper presented at the Annual Meeting of the American Political Science Association, New Orleans, Louisiana.

Kingson, Eric R. 1984. "Financing Social Security: Agenda-Setting and the Enactment of the 1983 Amendments to the Social Security Act." *Policy Studies Journal* 13: 131–55.

Klemmack, David L., and Lucinda L. Roff. 1980. "Public Support for Age as an Eligibility Criterion for Programs for Older Persons." *Gerontologist* 20: 148–53.

———. 1981. "Predicting General and Comparative Support for Government's Providing Benefits to Older Persons." *Gerontologist* 21: 592–99.

Kosterlitz, Julie. 1986a. "Getting Out Early." *National Journal* (October 4): 2374–78.

———. 1986b. "Protecting the Elderly." *National Journal* (May 24): 1254–58.

———. 1987a. "Health Care '88." *National Journal* (August 29): 2187.

———. Kosterlitz, Julie. 1987b. "Prescribing Pain." *National Journal* (July 18): 1845–48.

———. 1987c. "Test of Strength." *National Journal* (October 24): 2652–57.

Kuhn, Margaret E. 1976. "What Old People Want for Themselves and Others in Society." In Paul A. Kerschner, ed., *Advocacy and Age.* Los Angeles: Ethel Percy Andrus Gerontology Center, University of Southern California.

Lammers, William W. 1981. "Congress and the Aging." In Richard H. Davis, ed., *Aging: Prospects and Issues*, 3d ed. Los Angeles: Ethel Percy Andrus Gerontology Center, University of Southern California.

———. 1983. *Public Policy and the Aging.* Washington, D.C.: Congressional Quarterly Press.

Lazer, William. 1985. "Inside the Mature Market." *American Demographics* 7 (March): 22–27.

Lenkowsky, Leslie. 1987. "Why Growing Older Is Getting Better." *Public Opinion* 10 (May/June): 46–47.

Lichter, Linda S. 1985. "Who Speaks for Black America?" *Public Opinion* 8 (August/September): 41–44.

Light, Larry. 1981. "The Organized Elderly: A Powerful Lobby." *Congressional Quarterly Weekly Report* (November 28): 2345.

Light, Paul. 1985. *Artful Work: The Politics of Social Security Reform*. New York: Random House.

Linowes, David F., Harmon Zeigler, and Colin Bennett. 1983. "Overview: Interest Groups and Public Policy." *Policy Studies Journal* 11: 599–602.

Longman, Phillip. 1985. "Justice Between Generations." *The Atlantic Monthly* (June): 73–81.

Loomis, Burdett A. 1983. "A New Era: Groups and the Grass Roots." In Allan J. Cigler and Burdett A. Loomis, eds., *Interest Group Politics*. Washington, D.C.: Congressional Quarterly Press.

Lowi, Theodore J. 1964. "American Business, Public Policy, and Political Theory." *World Politics* 16: 677–715.

———. 1979. *The End of Liberalism: Ideology, Policy, and the Crisis of Public Authority*, 2d ed. New York: Norton.

Lowy, Louis. 1980. "Introduction." In Elizabeth W. Markson and Gretchen R. Batra, eds., *Public Policies for an Aging Population*. Lexington, Mass.: Lexington Books, D.C. Heath.

Lubove, Roy. 1986. *The Struggle for Social Security, 1900–1935*, 2d ed. Pittsburgh: University of Pittsburgh Press.

Margolis, Howard. 1982. *Selfishness, Altruism, and Rationality: A Theory of Social Choice*. Chicago: University of Chicago Press.

Marmor, Theodore R. 1973. *The Politics of Medicare*. Chicago: University of Chicago Press.

Mauss, Armand L. 1975. *Social Problems as Social Movements*. Philadelphia: J.B. Lippincott.

McClosky, Herbert. 1964. "Consensus and Ideology in American Politics." *American Political Science Review* 58: 361–82.

McConnell, Grant. 1966. *Private Power and American Democracy*. New York: Alfred A. Knopf.

McFarland, Andrew S. 1983. "Public Interest Lobbies Versus Minority Faction." In Allan J. Cigler and Burdett A. Loomis, eds., *Interest Group Politics*. Washington, D.C.: Congressional Quarterly Press.

———. 1984. *Common Cause: Lobbying in the Public Interest*. Chatham, N.J.: Chatham House Publishers.

———. 1987. "Interest Groups and Theories of Power in America." *British Journal of Political Science* 17: 129–47.

McLean, Iain, 1986. "Review Article: Some Recent Work in Public Choice." *British Journal of Political Science* 16: 377–94.

Meyers, Alan R. 1980. "Ethnicity and Aging: Public Policy and Ethnic Differences in Aging and Old Age." In Elizabeth W. Markson and Gretchen R. Batra, eds., *Public Policies for an Aging Population*. Lexington, Mass.: Lexington Books, D.C. Heath.

Michels, Robert. 1958 [1915]. *Political Parties*. New York: Free Press.

Miller, Arthur H., Patricia Gurin, and Gerald Gurin. 1980. "Age Consciousness and Political Mobilization of Older Americans." *Gerontologist* 20: 691–700.

Miller, Arthur H., Patricia Gurin, Gerald Gurin, and Oksana Malanchuk. 1981. "Group Consciousness and Political Participation." *American Journal of Political Science* 25: 494–511.

Miller, Stephen. 1983. *Special Interest Groups in American Politics*. New Brunswick: Transaction.

Miller, Warren E., and National Election Studies/Center for Political Studies. 1986. *American National Election Studies, 1976, 1978, 1980, 1982, 1984 and 1986*. Machine-readable data file. Ann Arbor: Inter-University Consortium for Political and Social Research, University of Michigan.

Mills, C. Wright. 1956. *The Power Elite*. New York: Oxford University Press.

Moe, Terry M. 1980. *The Organization of Interests*. Chicago: University of Chicago Press.

———. 1981. "Toward a Broader View of Interest Groups." *Journal of Politics* 43: 531–43.

Muller, Edward N., and Karl-Dieter Opp. 1986. "Rational Choice and Rebellious Collective Action." *American Political Science Review* 80: 471–87.

Myers, Frank E. 1976. "Civil Disobedience and Organisational Change: The British Committee of 100." In Richard Rose, ed., *Studies in British Politics: A Reader in Political Sociology*, 3d ed. New York: St. Martin's Press.

Myles, John F. 1983. "Comparative Public Policies for the Elderly: Frameworks and Resources for Analysis." In Anne-Marie Guillemard, ed., *Old Age and the Welfare State*. Beverly Hills: Sage.

———. 1984. "Conflict, Crisis and the Future of Old Age Security." In Meredith Minkler and Carroll L. Estes, eds., *Readings in the Political Economy of Aging*. Farmingdale, N.Y.: Baywood.

National Council on the Aging. 1975. *The Myth and Reality of Aging*. Washington, D.C.: The National Council on the Aging.

———. 1981. *Aging in the Eighties: America in Transition*. Washington, D.C.: The National Council on the Aging.

Nelson, Gary M. 1982. "Social Class and Public Policy for the Elderly." In Bernice L. Neugarten, ed., *Age or Need?* Beverly Hills: Sage.

Neugarten, Bernice L. 1982. "Age or Need?" *National Forum* 62 (Fall): 25–27.

Neugarten, Bernice L. and Gunhild O. Hagestad. 1976. "Age and the Life Course." In Robert H. Binstock and Ethel Shanas, eds., *Handbook of Aging and the Social Sciences*. New York: Van Nostrand Reinhold.

Nie, Norman H., Sidney Verba, and Jae-on Kim. 1974. "Political Participation and the Lifecycle." *Comparative Politics* 6: 319–40.

O'Gorman, Hubert J. 1980. "False Consciousness of Kind: Pluralistic Ignorance Among the Aged." *Research on Aging* 2: 105–28.

Olson, Laura Katz. 1982. *The Political Economy of Aging: The State, Private Power and Social Welfare*. New York: Columbia University Press.

Olson, Mancur, Jr. 1965. *The Logic of Collective Action*. Cambridge, Mass.: Harvard University Press.

Orloff, Ann Shola, and Theda Skocpol. 1984. "Why Not Equal Protection? Explaining the Politics of Public Social Spending in Britain, 1900–1911, and the United States, 1800s–1920." *American Sociological Review* 49: 726–50.

Ornstein, Norman J., and Shirley Elder. 1978. *Interest Groups, Lobbying and Policymaking*. Washington, D.C.: Congressional Quarterly Press.

Pateman, Carole. 1970. *Participation and Democratic Theory*. Cambridge: Cambridge University Press.

Peirce, Neal R., and Peter C. Choharis. 1982. "The Elderly as a Political Force—26 Million Strong and Well Organized." *National Journal* (September 11): 1559–62.

Peterson, Paul E. 1976. "British Interest Group Theory Re-Examined." In Richard Rose, ed., *Studies in British Politics: A Reader in Political Sociology*. New York: St. Martin's Press.

Pinner, Frank A., Paul Jacobs, and Philip Selznick. 1959. *Old Age and Political Behavior: A Case Study*. Berkeley: University of California Press.

Pitkin, Hanna F. 1967. *The Concept of Representation*. Berkeley: University of California Press.

———. 1969. "Introduction." In Hanna F. Pitkin, ed., *Representation*. New York: Atherton Press.

Polsby, Nelson W. 1980. *Community Power and Political Theory*, 2d ed. New Haven: Yale University Press.

———. 1983. *Consequences of Party Reform*. New York: Oxford University Press.

Ponza, Michael, Greg J. Duncan, Mary Corcoran, and Fred Groskind. 1988. "The Guns of Autumn? Age Differences in Support for Income Transfers to the Young and Old." *Public Opinion Quarterly* 52: 441–66.

Pratt, Henry J. 1974. "Old Age Associations in National Politics." *Annals of the American Academy of Political and Social Science* 415: 106–19.

———. 1976. *The Gray Lobby*. Chicago: University of Chicago Press.

———. 1978. "Symbolic Politics and White House Conferences on Aging." *Society* 15 (July/August): 67–72.

———. 1982. "The 'Gray Lobby' Revisited." *National Forum* 62 (Fall): 31–33.

———. 1983. "National Interest Groups Among the Elderly: Consolidation and Constraint." In William P. Browne and Laura Katz Olson, eds., *Aging and Public Policy: The Politics of Growing Old in America*. Westport, Conn.: Greenwood Press.

Punnett, R. M. 1971. *British Government and Politics*, 2d ed. New York: W. W. Norton.

Pynoos, Jon. 1984. "Setting the Elderly Housing Agenda." *Policy Studies Journal* 13: 173–84.

Ragan, Pauline K., and William J. Davis. 1978. "The Diversity of Older Voters." *Society* 15 (July/August): 50–53.

Ragan, Pauline K., and James J. Dowd. 1974. "The Emerging Political Consciousness of the Aged: A Generation Interpretation." *Journal of Social Issues* 30: 137–58.

Rauch, Jonathan. 1987. "The Politics of Joy." *National Journal* (January 17): 125–30.

Rhodebeck, Laurie A. 1985. "Group Identifications and Policy Preferences: A Reformulation of Group Influence Models." Paper presented at the Annual Meeting of the American Political Science Association, New Orleans.

Riche, Martha Farnsworth. 1985. "The Oldest Old." *American Demographics* 7 (November): 44–45.

Riley, Matilda White. 1973. "Aging and Cohort Succession: Interpretations and Misinterpretations." *Public Opinion Quarterly* 37: 35–49.

Rose, Arnold M. 1965a. "Group Consciousness Among the Aged." In Arnold M. Rose and Warren A. Peterson, eds., *Older People and their Social World*. Philadelphia: F.A. Davis.

———. 1965b. "The Structure of the Aging: A Framework for Research in Social Gerontology." In Arnold M. Rose and Warren A. Peterson, eds., *Older People and their Social World*. Philadelphia: F.A. Davis.

Rosenbaum, Walter A., and James W. Button. 1987. "The Aging in Sunbelt Communities: Political Participation in Local Politics." Paper presented at the Annual Meeting of the American Political Science Association, Chicago, Illinois.

Rovner, Julie. 1987. "House OKs Medicare Expansion Despite Reservations Over Cost." *Congressional Quarterly Weekly Report* (July 25): 1637–42.

———. 1988a. "Catastrophic Costs Conferees Irked by Lobbying Assaults." *Congressional Quarterly Weekly Report* (March 26): 777–80.

———. 1988b. "Long-Term Care Bill Derailed—For Now." *Congressional Quarterly Weekly Report* (June 11): 1604–5.

Salisbury, Robert H. 1969. "An Exchange Theory of Interest Groups." *Midwest Journal of Political Science* 13: 1–32.

———. 1975. "Interest Groups." In Fred I. Greenstein and Nelson W. Polsby, eds., *Handbook of Political Science*, Vol. 4, "Nongovernmental Politics." Reading, Mass.: Addison-Wesley.

———. 1983. "Interest Groups: Toward a New Understanding." In Allan J. Cigler and Burdett A. Loomis, eds., *Interest Group Politics*. Washington, D.C.: Congressional Quarterly Press.

Samuelson, Robert J. 1981. "Benefit Programs for the Elderly—Off Limits to Federal Budget Cutters?" *National Journal* (October 3): 1757–62.

Sartori, Giovanni. 1962. *Democratic Theory*. Detroit: Wayne State University.

———. 1968. "Representation: Representational Systems." In David L. Sills, ed., *International Encyclopedia of the Social Sciences*, Vol. 13. New York: Macmillan/Free Press.

Schattschneider, E. E. 1960. *The Semisovereign People*. New York: Holt, Rinehart and Winston.

Schlozman, Kay Lehman, and John T. Tierney. 1986. *Organized Interests and American Democracy.* New York: Harper & Row.

Schreiber, E. M., and Lorna R. Marsden. 1972. "Age and Opinions on a Government Program of Medical Aid." *Journal of Gerontology* 27: 95–101.

Schulz, James H. 1988. *The Economics of Aging,* 4th ed. Dover, Mass.: Auburn House.

Scott, W. Richard. 1981. "Reform Movements and Organizations: The Case of Aging." In Sara B. Keisler, James N. Morgan, and Valerie Kincaid Oppenheimer, eds., *Aging: Social Change.* New York: Academic Press.

Shapiro, Robert Y., and Tom W. Smith. "The Polls: Social Security." *Public Opinion Quarterly* 49: 561–72.

Simpson, Richard L., and William H. Gulley. 1973. "Goals, Environmental Pressures, and Organizational Characteristics." In Wolf V. Heydebrand, ed., *Comparative Organizations: The Results of Empirical Research.* Englewood Cliffs, N.J.: Prentice-Hall.

Smeeding, Timothy. 1986. "Nonmoney Income and the Elderly: The Case of the 'Tweeners.' " *Journal of Policy Analysis and Management* 5: 707–24.

Smeeding, Timothy, and Barbara Boyle Torrey. 1987. "The Economic Status of the Old in Six Countries." Paper presented at the annual meeting of the Population Association of America.

Smith, John Patrick, and Oscar B. Martinson. 1984. "Socio-Political Bases of Senior Citizen Mobilization: Salient Issues Beyond Health Policy." *Research on Aging* 6: 213–24.

Spitler, B. J. Curry. 1981. "Policies Affecting Older Americans." In Richard H. Davis, ed., *Aging: Prospects and Issues,* 3d ed. Los Angeles: Ethel Percy Andrus Gerontology Center, University of Southern California.

Stockman, David A. 1987. *The Triumph of Politics,* 2d ed. New York: Avon.

Storey, James R. 1983. *Older Americans in the Reagan Era: Impacts of Federal Policy Changes.* Washington, D.C.: Urban Institute Press.

Tocqueville, Alexis de. 1945. *Democracy in America.* New York: Alfred A. Knopf.

Torres-Gil, Fernando M. 1982. *Politics of Aging Among Elder Hispanics.* Washington, D.C.: University Press of America.

———. 1986. "The Latinization of a Multigenerational Population: Hispanics in an Aging Society." *Daedalus* 115: 325–48.

Trela, James E. 1972. "Age Structure of Voluntary Associations and Political Self-Interest Among the Aged." Sociological Quarterly 13: 244–52.

———. 1976. "Social Class and Association Membership." *Journal of Gerontology* 31: 198–203.

Truman, David B. 1971. *The Governmental Process,* 2d ed. New York: Alfred A. Knopf.

U.S. Bureau of the Census. 1975. *Historical Statistics of the United States, Colonial Times to 1970, Bicentennial Edition.* Washington, D.C.: U.S. Government Printing Office.

———. 1983. *America in Transition: An Aging Society.* Current Population

Reports, Series P–23, No. 128. Washington, D.C.: U.S. Government Printing Office.

———. 1984. *Projections of the Population by Age, Sex, and Race: 1983 to 2080.* Current Population Reports, Series, P-25, No. 952. Washington, D.C.: U.S. Government Printing Office.

———. 1986. *Household Wealth and Asset Ownership: 1984.* Current Population Reports, Series P-70, No. 7. Washington, D.C.: U.S. Government Printing Office.

———. 1987a. *Estimates of Poverty Including the Value of Noncash Benefits: 1986.* Technical Paper 57. Washington, D.C.: U.S. Government Printing Office.

———. 1987b. *Money Income and Poverty Status of Families and Persons in the United States: 1986.* Current Population Reports, Series P-60, No. 157. Washington, D.C.: U.S. Government Printing Office.

———. 1987c. *Statistical Abstract of the United States.* Washington, D.C.: U.S. Bureau of the Census.

———. 1988. *Money Income and Poverty Status of Families and Persons in the United States: 1987.* Current Population Reports, Series P-60, No. 161. Washington, D.C.: U.S. Government Printing Office.

U.S. Senate, Special Committee on Aging. 1984. *Older Americans and the Federal Budget: Past, Present, and Future.* Washington, D.C.: U.S. Government Printing Office.

U.S. Senate, Special Committee on Aging, and the American Association of Retired Persons. 1984. *Aging America: Trends and Projections.* Washington, D.C.: U.S. Government Printing Office.

Verba, Sidney, and Norman H. Nie. 1972. *Participation in America.* New York: Harper & Row.

Villers Foundation. 1987. *On the Other Side of Easy Street: Myths and Facts about the Economics of Old Age.* Washington, D.C.: Villlers Foundation.

Vinyard, Dale. 1973. "The Senate Committee on the Aging and the Development of a Policy System." *Michigan Academician* 5: 281–94.

———. 1978. "The Rediscovery of the Elderly." *Society* 15 (July/August): 24–29.

———. 1979. "The House Select Committee on the Aging." *Long Term Care and Health Services Administration Quarterly* 3: 317–24.

———. 1983. "Public Policy and Institutional Politics." In William P. Browne and Laura Katz Olson, eds., *Aging and Public Policy: The Politics of Growing Old in America.* Westport, Conn.: Greenwood Press.

Vogel, David. 1980–81. "The Public-Interest Movement and the American Reform Tradition." *Political Science Quarterly* 95: 607–27.

Wahlke, John C., Heniz Eulau, William Buchanan, and LeRoy C. Ferguson. 1962. *The Legislative System: Explorations in Legislative Behavior.* New York: John Wiley and Sons.

Walker, Jack L. 1983. "The Origins and Maintenance of Interest Groups in America." *American Political Science Review* 77: 390–406.

Ward, Russell A. 1977. "Aging Group Consciousness: Implications in an Older Sample." *Sociology and Social Research* 61: 496–519.

Weaver, Jerry L. 1976. "The Elderly as a Political Community." *Western Political Quarterly* 29: 610–19.

—————. 1981. "Issue Salience: The Elderly as a Political Community: The Case of National Health Policy." In Robert B. Hudson, ed., *The Aging in Politics*. Springfield, Ill.: William C. Thomas.

Weissman, Harold H. 1970. *Community Councils and Community Control: The Working of a Democratic Mythology*. Pittsburgh: University of Pittsburgh Press.

Williamson, John B., Linda Evans, and Lawrence A. Powell. 1982. *The Politics of Aging: Power and Policy*. Springfield, Ill.: Charles C. Thomas.

Wilson, Graham K. 1981. *Interest Groups in the United States*. New York: Oxford University Press.

Wilson, James Q. 1973. *Political Organizations*. New York: Basic Books.

Wolfinger, Raymond E. 1974. *The Politics of Progress*. Englewood Cliffs, N.J.: Prentice-Hall.

Wolfinger, Raymond E., and Steven J. Rosenstone. 1980. *Who Votes?* New Haven: Yale University Press.

Zald, Mayer N., and John D. McCarthy, eds. 1979. *The Dynamics of Social Movements: Resource Mobilization, Social Control, and Tactics*. Cambridge: Winthrop.

Zeigler, Harmon, and Keith Poole. 1985. "Political Woman: Gender Indifference." *Public Opinion* 8 (August/September): 54–56.